OSPREY AIRCRAFT OF THE ACE

Morane-Saulnier MS.406 Aces

SERIES EDITOR: TONY HOLMES

OSPREY AIRCRAFT OF THE ACES 121

Morane-Saulnier MS.406 Aces

Christian-Jacques Ehrengardt and Kari Stenman

OSPREY
PUBLISHING

Front Cover
Formed in December 1939, GC III/1 had few opportunities to clash with the Luftwaffe during the 'Phoney War' period. However, when the *Blitzkrieg* commenced on 10 May 1940, pilots from the unit were roused from their sleep at 0400 hrs by a low-flying aircraft that they misidentified as Junkers Ju 88. It was in fact a Heinkel He 111P of 3./KG 27, which strafed the airfield at Norrent-Fontes and fled before a patrol of MS.406s was scrambled. Among the French pilots who took off as the day was dawning was Sgt Kléber Doublet.

In the meantime, more He 111s of KG 27 appeared over Norrent-Fontes and were immediately attacked by the French fighters.

Having been unable to stay in formation due to mechanical problems, Doublet missed the melee that ensued over the airfield, but he was able to chase down the lone 'Ju 88' that had initially attacked Norrent-Fontes, this aircraft remaining in the area to check on the results of the bombing by the main formation from KG 27. Doublet made several passes from dead astern, avoiding the return fire from the gunners and probably killing one of them. The He 111 subsequently performed a wheel-up landing near Hazebrouck at 0520 hrs, with one member of its crew having been killed. The remainder were captured, including Hauptmann Dr Walter-Julius Bloehm, a then famous novelist and screenwriter. He was duly released in late June 1940 following the French capitulation, and ended the war with the rank of major, having served in various headquarters.

Kléber Doublet was mortally wounded on 11 June 1940 when the engine of his MS.406 engine refused to start after GC III/1 had been ordered to retreat to Valence, in southern France. He was still standing by his crippled Morane when German bombers arrived overhead, targeting Rozay-en-Brie airfield. Doublet suffered terrible wounds to both of his legs, the six-victory ace succumbing to his injuries the next day in hospital. (*Cover artwork by Mark Postlethwaite*)

First published in Great Britain in 2014 by Osprey Publishing
PO Box 883, Oxford, OX1 9PL, UK
PO Box 3985, New York, NY 10185-3985, USA

E-mail: info@ospreypublishing.com

Osprey Publishing is part of the Osprey Group

© 2014 Osprey Publishing Limited

A CIP catalogue record for this book is available from the British Library

ISBN: 978 1 78200 341 0
PDF e-book ISBN: 978 1 78200 342 7
ePub ISBN: 978 1 78200 343 4

Edited by Tony Holmes and Philip Jarrett
Cover Artwork by Mark Postlethwaite
Aircraft Profiles by Chris Davey
Index by Zoe Ross
Originated by PDQ Digital Media Solutions, UK
Printed in China through Asia Pacific Offset Limited

14 15 16 17 18   10 9 8 7 6 5 4 3 2 1

Osprey Publishing is supporting the Woodland Trust, the UK's leading woodland conservation charity, by funding the dedication of trees.

www.ospreypublishing.com

Previous Spread
A *patrouille* of MS.406s from GC II/3 prepares to take off from Connantre on a patrol over the Franco-German border in March 1940 (*via Author*)

Back Cover
MS.406s of 1/LeLv 28 at Ladva forward landing ground, north of the River Svir, in September 1943. The aircraft are, from the left, MS-619 and MS-643. This base completely escaped detection by Soviet aerial reconnaissance, and the 1st Flight was able to operate undetected for its whole three months' stay there (*SA-kuva*)

CONTENTS

INTRODUCTION

The Morane-Saulnier MS.406 was an important aircraft not only because of the sheer number produced (more than 1000 had been built when France went out of the war in June 1940), but also because it was the first really modern fighter in the *Armée de l'Air* (French Air Force) inventory. Although it was comparable with the British Hawker Hurricane and early models of the German Messerschmitt Bf 109, it could not hold its own against the more powerful Bf 109E and Bf 110C.

The MS.406 was the mainstay of the *Armée de l'Air* during the 'Phoney War', but it had begun to be phased out in favour of the more potent Dewoitine D.520 at the turn of 1940. However, owing to the limited capacities of the French aircraft industry, five of the twelve units that started the war with Moranes had to carry on until the bitter end with the same type.

With no protection, the MS.406 sustained heavy losses during the Battle of France. It was slow and too lightly armed with unreliable weapons, so bringing down the fast German bombers was no easy task, let alone engaging in dogfights with the Bf 109, which outperformed it in all respects except for manoeuvrability. But, as one pilot put it, 'Turning does not win a dogfight'. Therefore, it comes as no surprise that only 12 French pilots became fully fledged aces at the controls of the MS.406 during this period, although many kills were shared.

However, a score of others, who notched their very first kills at the controls of the Morane, fought the rest of World War 2 flying D.520s, Supermarine Spitfires and even Soviet Yakovlevs to attain 'acedom' against opponents whose aircraft bore black crosses, white stars or red-white-and-blue roundels.

It is a little-known fact that, although the MS.406 was phased out in non-occupied France and northern Africa after the armistice was signed with Germany in June 1940, it soldiered on to protect French colonies that remained under the control of the Vichy government. The Morane was briefly pitted against the Japanese and the Thais in French Indochina in late 1940, against the Commonwealth air forces in Syria during May-June 1941 and over Madagascar in 1942.

It was also used by the Croatian Air Force and on a larger scale by the *Ilmavoimat* (Finnish Air Force), whose operations are dealt with in the second part of this book.

'THE BEST FIGHTER IN THE WORLD'

The Morane-Saulnier MS.405 was designed to a specification issued in 1934, calling for a fighter able to achieve 400 km/h (250 mph) in level flight. Departing from their typical braced parasol monoplanes, the design team led by Paul-René Gauthier came up with a cantilevered low-wing monoplane. However, it retained the fabric-covered steel framework of the classic biplanes of the 1930s (except for the metal-covered forward fuselage), but incorporated 'novel' features such as a retractable undercarriage, an enclosed cockpit, landing flaps and a variable-pitch propeller – equipment usually regarded by 'old-time' pilots as 'gadgets'.

Considered an interim fighter until more advanced types came off the drawing boards, the MS.405 was built around the Hispano-Suiza 12Ygrs 12-cylinder liquid-cooled engine, which produced 860 hp at an altitude of 4000 m (13,000 ft). It was to be armed with one 20 mm Hispano S7 cannon mounted between the cylinder banks and firing through the propeller hub, and two drum-fed 7.5 mm MAC 1934 machine guns in the wings.

The prototype, MS.405-01, made its maiden flight on 8 August 1935, and after official trials a pre-production batch of 15 machines was ordered, the first one being delivered in August 1936. The basic design was sound, with no vices, the aircraft being easy to fly and highly manoeuvrable.

However, it was not devoid of defects, none of which would be eradicated. In particular, the semi-retractable ventral radiator was the source of many problems. When lowered it caused pronounced drag that dramatically reduced the top speed, and when it was raised the engine overheated so much that it could not be pushed to its full power. The undercarriage, having no locking device, was prone to lower in hard turns or dive recoveries – no small handicap in a dogfight. As the

When it was displayed at the international meeting at Bruxelles-Evère in July 1937, the MS.405 was hailed as the 'best fighter in the word' – a superlative that could never have been applied to its successor, the MS 406. Like all French fighters of this era, the latter machine lacked a truly powerful engine such as the German Daimler-Benz DB 601 or the British Rolls-Royce Merlin, both of which developed around 20 per cent more horsepower than the French Hispano-Suiza (*via Author*)

official technical services did not consider it essential to provide heating for the wing machine guns, they froze above 4000 m (13,000 ft), which was the usual combat altitude in 1940. Like all combat aircraft of its era, the MS.405-01 had no armour (not even an armoured windshield) and no self-sealing tanks, and its complex and vulnerable electrical and hydraulic systems would prove to be another Achilles' heel.

In June 1937 the MS.405-01 was displayed by the famous aerobatic pilot Michel Détroyat at the international meeting at Bruxelles-Evère, where it was optimistically presented as 'the best fighter in the world'. It might not have been the best, but it was surely one of the fastest, as Détroyat returned to the Morane plant at Puteaux, near Paris, at an average speed of 430 km/h (270 mph) – quite an achievement at that time. Alas, the reputation was short-lived.

The proposed version to be mass-built was the MS.406, powered by a Hispano-Suiza 12Y31, its variable-pitch Chauvière 351 propeller soon being replaced by a constant-speed Ratier 1607. MS.406 No 1 first flew on 20 May 1938. The *Armée de l'Air* was lagging so far behind in re-equipping its fighter units with modern types that no fewer than 1082 MS.406s were ordered within a few weeks. Production had to be split between several recently nationalised companies, and 11 factories were to manufacture parts to be assembled by the *Société Nationale de Constructions Aéronautiques de l'Ouest* (SNCAO) at Nantes-Bouguenais. A grand total of 1077 (this number is still an issue for debate) MS.406s were taken on charge by the *Armée de l'Air* before the armistice of June 1940.

However, despite its simple structure the MS.406 required twice as many man-hours as the Bf 109 to be assembled (the Bf 109 took 1600 hours) – as many as the Spitfire I, which was reputed to be an industrial nightmare to build. This further delayed French fighter units' conversion to the type. Moreover, companies manufacturing essential parts such as propellers and gunsights created bottlenecks because of their low output.

Fresh from the factory, two MS.406s rev up on the SNCASO tarmac before their maiden flights in May 1939. Closest to the camera is Nº244, which was allocated to GC II/2 and lost to flak on 8 June 1940 (its pilot, Adj Jacques Marconnet, was killed). The aviator seen here securing his helmet is Michel Détroyat, Morane-Saulnier's chief test pilot and a renowned aerobatic pilot (*via Author*)

Some early pre-series machines were allocated to the 4th *Escadrille* of *Groupe de Chasse* (GC) II/7 (the basic organisation of French units is given in Appendix 1) at Dijon for operational evaluation in late 1938. The first production MS.406 was delivered in September 1938, and in early 1939 the 6th and 7th *Escadres de Chasse* began their conversions. When France declared war on Germany on 3 September 1939, 347 of the 573 machines taken on charge by the *Armée de l'Air* equipped ten fiontline *Groupes de Chasse* based on French metropolitan soil as follows;

GC I/2	Beauvais-Tillé
GC II/2	Clermont-les-Fermes
GC III/2	Cambrai-Niergnies
GC I/3	Velaine-en-Haye
GC II/3	Fayence
GC III/3	Salon-de-Provence
GC II/6	Anglure-Vouarces
GC III/6	Villacoublay
GC II/7	Luxeuil-Saint-Sauveur
GC III/7	Ambérieu

DERIVATIVES

The basic MS.406 gave birth to many different versions, but none of them reached operational status, at least in France, and they will not be dealt with in detail in this volume. The most promising was probably the MS.410, equipped with a fixed radiator, four belt-fed wing guns, jet exhaust pipes and the provision for two underwing 140-litre (30.8 gallon) ferrying tanks. It was planned to modify 621 MS.406s into this new configuration, but the scheme was delayed due to SNCAO's heavy commitment to production of the MS.406 and the Lioré-et-Olivier LeO 451. The first machine, No 1035, flew in April 1940. The German onslaught a few weeks later led to the abandonment of the programme. Most MS.406s earmarked for conversion were sent back to frontline units to make up for the heavy losses sustained in combat, with only 12 aircraft actually being modified. With the type already being obsolescent prior to its introduction to service, the MS.410 would have made no significant difference for the *Armée de l'Air's* struggle with the Luftwaffe.

Several foreign countries were interested in acquiring the type, but none were delivered because of the embargo imposed on arms exports when France went to war. However, 40 MS.406s were shipped to Turkey in an attempt to gain the favour of this neutral country. Switzerland built the D-3801 and D-3802 under licence, these being similar, respectively, to the MS.411 and MS.450, which did not progress beyond the first prototype stage in France.

THE PHONEY WAR

War had not yet broken out when disaster struck GC III/3. On 28 August 1939, while transferring from Dijon to Salon-de-Provence, the unit's pilots became lost in a heavy fog. Seven Moranes hit the ground, resulting in three pilots being killed and four injured. Strict censorship concealed this tragedy from the press, and it was only revealed long after the war. Marcel Soulages, then a sergent in the 6th *Escadrille*, had a close shave, as he recalled;

'About ten minutes after takeoff we met a heavy blanket of fog that seemed to stretch from one side of the horizon to the other, but, high above, the sky was still blue with good visibility. At this moment Cne Travers [CO of GC III/3] said his oil pressure had dropped and left command of the unit in the hands of his deputy, Cne Monjean, before turning back. Unfortunately, the latter had not planned the flight and was caught off guard. Unable to locate the direction of Salon-de-Provence from above the fog, he decided to fly under it so as to navigate visually. By waving his wings he gave the order to tighten up the formations and then dived steadfastly towards the ground.

'As far as our section was concerned, we were already flying in close formation — i.e. 50 cm [20 in] behind our leader's wing and, like all others, we entered this thick fog. My altimeter was reading 400 m [1300 ft]. However close I was to him, I suddenly lost sight of my leader. I applied hard rudder to break off, and all of a sudden I saw a dark halo ahead of me and instinctively I pulled as hard as I could on my stick. I was just in time, as I missed the top of a tree by just inches. I pulled up a little more and eventually reached the clear blue sky out in the sun.'

An investigation took place after this incident but no pilot was ever asked to testify, and its conclusions were never disclosed. Soulages shared in the destruction of a Bf 109 on 30 September 1939, but suffering from heart disease following an oxygen failure in December 1939, he ended up being relegated to role of an instructor.

At the outbreak of war the *Armée de l'Air* had only two modern fighter types in its inventory, the Curtiss H-75A and the MS.406. The first one to clash with the Luftwaffe was the American-built aircraft on 8 September 1939 (see Osprey Aircraft of the Aces 86 – *P-36 Hawk Aces of World War 2* for further details).

Thirteen days later nine Moranes of GC I/3 provided the escort for an antiquated Potez 390 that had been tasked with undertaking a reconnaissance mission of the

Sgt Marcel Soulages (left) and his mechanic pose in front of MS.406 N°467 at Dijon-Longvic some time before tragedy struck GC III/3 on 28 August 1939 (*via Author*)

Five pilots of GC I/3 pose for war correspondents after their successful combat on 24 September 1939 against Bf 109Ds of JGr. 152. They are, from left to right, Sous-Lt Pierre Salva, Sous-Lt Lucien Potier, Cne Bernard Challe, Sgt Chaussat and Sgt-chef Jean Octave. Bernard Challe claimed five victories in the May-June campaign, and Salva four, all of them while flying the D.520 (*via Author*)

Wiesbaden area. They were bounced by Bf 109Es from JG 53, which damaged the observation aircraft so badly that it was forced down behind French lines. Hauptmann Dr Erich Mix of *Stab* I./JG 53 set Sous-Lt Marius Baizé's MS.406 on fire, and although the Frenchman managed to bail out, flames from the aircraft had spread to his parachute and he was killed when he fell into a river. At that time Mix was the mayor of the city of Wiesbaden – he had found a unique way to protect his fellow citizens! Baizé was the first Morane pilot killed in action.

On 24 September GC I/3 took its revenge when a section of four Moranes clashed with six Bf 109Ds of JGr. 152 near Saarbrücken. The French pilots lost their leader, Cne Roger Gérard, who was able to take to his parachute, but not before despatching one of his opponents. Sgt Jean Garnier was wounded during the Messerschmitts' first attack, and when he broke off and landed on an auxiliary airfield at Etting he was killed when a Bf 109 that had followed him down strafed his Morane on the ground. Despite being set upon by German fighters, Adj-chef Antonin Combette managed to bring down a Bf 109. Upon Combette's return to Velaine-en-Haye, his mechanics counted 28 bullet holes in his MS.406.

The two German pilots that had been shot down were taken prisoner, and Leutnant Kurt Rosenkranz was invited to lunch by his victor, Cne Gérard. Rosenkranz's fighter was the first of the four kills Gérard would claim during the 1939-40 period. Born in 1898, Gérard had been credited with a probable victory on 30 October 1918 while flying with one of the famous *Cigogne* (Stork) units on the Western Front. After a gallant campaign in May-June 1940 he returned to civilian life in August of that year and fought on with the Resistance.

Gérard's family ran a foundry near Lyon and on his request they had supplied him with five-millimetre-thick (quarter-inch) steel plates to protect the seats of GC I/3's Moranes – it had been proven that both Baizé and Garnier had been hit in the back while engaging Bf 109s in combat.

The clash on 24 September had effectively ended in a draw, with two machines destroyed and one damaged on either side. Morale was still high among French fighter units at this early stage of the conflict, as Pierre Salva, a former sous-lieutenant with GC I/3, noted;

'Our Moranes have not been outperformed by the Me 109s. Though much slower, they held their own thanks to their better manoeuvrability. While awaiting aircraft that will replace them – one which is much in the news is being built at Toulouse and called the Dewoitine 520; fast, manoeuvrable and well armed, in other words the ideal fighter – our Moranes will play their part without giving their pilots the feeling they have been sacrificed.'

Due to the need to protect the French border, which extended from Dunkirk in the north to Switzerland in the south, fighter units had to be spread out all along the 800 km (500 mile) front, and many were not to see a Luftwaffe aeroplane (apart from high-flying and fast reconnaissance aircraft that they could not catch) before the German onslaught of 10 May 1940. The 'hottest' areas were allocated to the Curtiss units, with most Morane groups being based where nothing happened. They therefore had fewer opportunities to clash with the Luftwaffe. For instance, GC III/3, which had been re-formed after the tragedy of late August, saw only two combats during the Phoney War – the first on 30 September 1939, when H-75As also saw much action in the skies of Alsace and Lorraine.

That day, while escorting a Potez 637 to Wissemburg, four Moranes of GC I/3 and three from GC III/3 were attacked by Bf 109s over Entsheim. Sgt Marcel Soulages damaged a Messerschmitt from 3./JG 53, and the fighter was polished off by his *chef de patrouille*, Adj Michel Marias. The latter's aircraft was damaged in return and his other wingman, Lt Pierre Patroux, was wounded in the arm and had to make an emergency landing in a field. The MS.406s of GC I/3 were unable to lend a hand or to protect the twin-engined reconnaissance aircraft, which was badly shot up. Marias, who would become a test pilot after the war with the rank of lieutenant colonel, recalled his first combat as follows;

'I returned in a bullet-riddled aircraft and landed on GC I/3's airfield at Toul-Velaine. Bullets had penetrated my parachute and one of them had brushed my spine. I found it between my flightsuit and my belt, and I kept it as a souvenir.'

Marias subsequently claimed two more victories in May 1940.

October and November were less turbulent in the air, mainly for climatic reasons and also because it was now obvious that no offensive would take place before the spring. Indeed, only two Henschel Hs 126s were claimed by Morane units in October.

On 9 November GC II/7 entered the field, chasing, but not destroying, a Dornier Do 17 whose gunner fought back vigorously. Twice he hit Sgt Pierre Boillot, fortunately with no consequences. Boillot, aged 21, had been posted to the *Groupe* six months earlier fresh from flying school. His comments about the *Armée de l'Air* Headquarters at this time were rather pointed;

'The first time I ever pressed the trigger was when I had a German aeroplane in my gunsight. I had never shot a round during my training time! Needless to say, the Dornier escaped unscathed. Sending pilots into battle without any actual aerial gunnery training was thoroughly unacceptable from an Air Command worthy of the name. The closest I came to aerial gunnery practice was two months after my arrival, when my *Groupe* was sent to a firing range in southern France. However, I was told by my CO, who thought that rookies were more of a pain in the arse than anything else, that I was not trained enough. So I remained at Dijon, spending a full month surveying the calisthenics of young Tommies instead of flying!'

As we shall see later, Boillot did train and improve his shooting abilities, ending the war with nine victories to his name. By an ironic twist of fate, immediately after World War 2 had ended Boillot was posted to the gunnery school at Salon-de-Provence as an instructor.

The next big clash between the Luftwaffe and Moranes occured on 22 November, when four MS.406s of GC II/7 caught a lone Do 17P of 4.(F)/121 over Moos. The pilot of the German reconnaissance aircraft was given no opportunity to escape, and crash-landed in his own lines at Sulzburg. The victory was shared by the four pilots involved, including two future leading figures of the *Armée de l'Air* in Adj-chef Georges Valentin and Sous-Lt Gabriel Gauthier, who would both claim ten victories during the war. Jacques Lamblin, a sergent-chef of the Reserve, and Sous-Lt Michel Gruyelle were also credited with the first victories of the four that they both would each eventually claim.

At 1115 hrs that same day the skies over Saarbrücken filled with French aircraft. No fewer than 21 Moranes were in the air, with six from GC I/3 protecting a lone Potez 63.11 and six from GC II/6 and nine from GC III/7 escorting ANF Les Mureaux 115 parasol-winged observation aeroplanes. At around 1140 hrs the Messerschmitts arrived. Six Bf 109Es of I./JG 76 dived on GC I/3, prompting GC II/6 to join in the fray. One Morane was badly damaged, but two Bf 109s were brought down, both landing in good condition behind French lines. The two German pilots were taken prisoner. One Bf 109 was subsequently displayed on the Champs-Élysées in Paris, the other being test-flown by the French before being sent to the Aeroplane and Armament Experimental Establishment at Boscombe Down in England, where it was given the British military serial AE479. One Bf 109 was credited to no fewer than eight pilots (see Appendix 2) and the other to two, including Sous-Lt Léon Cuffaut (GC II/6), another future great of French military aviation.

Cuffaut's career in the 1939-40 campaign ended when he was transferred as an instructor to the *Centre d'Instruction à la Chasse* at Chartres (similar to a RAF Operational Training Unit) in early 1940. After joining the *Normandie-Niémen* – the Free French unit that had been fighting on the Soviet side since April 1943 – Cuffaut added ten more kills to his tally. He subsequently flew combat missions

Sous-Lt Léon Cuffaut stands in front of a Morane of GC II/6 during the Phoney War. When fuselage roundels were introduced on French aircraft in March 1940, unit insignia were relegated to the fin, although many *Escadrilles* elected to keep them on the fuselage, albeit in a smaller size (*Service Historique de la Défense (SHD)/Air*)

in French Indochina between July 1953 and September 1955, and was the only French pilot to attain the 1000 operational sorties mark, actually flying 1010 in 2626 operational flying hours. Post-war, Col Cuffaut became the director of the *Aéro-Club de France*, a highly regarded organisation that registers all aviation world records.

However, aerial action for 22 November 1939 was not yet over, as more Moranes appeared over the frontline. Struggling with I./JG 51, GC III/7 lost one MS.406 but shot up a Bf 109. On their way home the Morane pilots encountered III./JG 53. Adj Albert Littolff had some trouble shaking off a Bf 109 that was sitting on his tail, finally landing his badly damaged aircraft at Azelot. The future Free French ace (14 victories) would enjoy better luck later in the campaign.

Gabriel Gauthier (centre) was one of several pilots from GC II/7 who ended their career with the rank of full general. He claimed most of his ten victories while flying Spitfires over Corsica and Germany. Gauthier flew with GC II/7 for more than six years, from October 1938 until June 1945 (*SHD/Air*)

The following day a *patrouille simple* (see Appendix 1) of GC III/6 found a lone Do 17P and shot it down at Bras-sur-Meuse. The victory was shared by Sgt-chef Pierre Le Gloan (the first of the 18 enemy aircraft he would eventually claim during the war) and Sous-Lt Robert Martin.

Almost a full month elapsed before MS.406s again saw some action. On 21 December 12 Moranes of GC II/7 on an escort mission for a Potez 63.11 between Karlsruhe and Aachen were intercepted by ten Bf 109Es belonging to the newly formed I./JG 54. As six Messerschmitts tried to attack the Potez, the rest engaged the Moranes. Having been separated from his section during the melee, Sous-Lt Gabriel Gauthier went after two Bf 109s on his own;

'I picked up the closest and opened fire at 50 m [55 yds], seeing pieces ripped off its tail. The pilot bailed out and I watched his aeroplane crash near Sponeck. But I had not noticed another "Monsieur Schmitt" [one of the nicknames given by the French to the Bf 109, another being "bouts carrés", referring to their squared wingtips] that had crept behind me. I only became aware of his presence when all hell broke loose in the cockpit. Instruments were smashed, debris and shrapnel flew all around me and then I was hit in the head. Blood began to flow over my face and I lost consciousness. I came back to life at 100 m [330 ft] – just in time to pull up and avoid striking the ground. My strength grew dim and I had lost the use of my left arm. I thought I would never be able to reach my airfield, so I opted for a belly landing in an open pasture. I fainted again and I woke up only to discover that I was in a hospital. The war was over for me.'

Gabriel Gauthier, known as 'Gégé' in the *Armée de l'Air* because he used to paint his initials on his aircraft, returned to GC II/7 in Tunisia a year later. He duly gained eight victories flying Spitfires after the ex-Vichy Air Force switched to the Allied side following Operation *Torch*. Shot down by flak, he evaded capture and returned via Switzerland. Gauthier rose to the rank of *général d'armée aérienne* (equivalent to full General in the US Air Force) and was chief of staff of the *Armée de l'Air* when he retired in 1972.

There was little action for the Morane units during the first three months of 1940, with only a handful of fighters being written off or damaged in clashes with Bf 109s over the front on 3 and 10 January and 2, 3, 9 and 25 March. However, on 31 March disaster struck GC III/7.

Eleven Moranes were despatched over the Morhange area, the fighters splitting up into four *patrouilles* at four different levels. The top cover at 6000 m (19,700 ft) was comprised of six aircraft under Cne Georges Lacombe. At one point Lacombe's oxygen supply broke down. Afraid he might faint, he suddenly went into a steep dive, hoping to fix the problem at 4000 m (13,000 ft). Not having the slightest idea of what was going on, all of his wingmen pushed their control columns forward in a 'follow-the-leader' reflex action. This most unfortunate move completely disrupted the whole formation.

At this very moment no fewer than 20 Bf 109s from II./JG 53 appeared on the scene and bounced the French aircraft at the worst possible time. The fight did not last more than a few minutes, but it was a massacre. Two pilots were killed, one bailed out severely burned, two were wounded and two other aircraft were damaged. At no time did the Morane pilots have any opportunity to fight back. This action was an ominous portent of things to come.

As it built up momentum the Luftwaffe became more and more aggressive with the passage of time. Rather than providing passive escorts for reconnaissance aircraft, German fighters were now taking the initiative over French soil in *freie Jagd* sweeps. Only the H-75As could take up the gauntlet, but they were too few in number, and the new modern French-made fighters such as the Bloch MB.152 and the Dewoitine

This MS.406, N°806, was usually flown by Cne Pierre Bouvarre, CO of the 6th *Escadrille* of GC III/7. However, on 31 March 1940 another pilot was at the controls when it was damaged by Bf 109s. Noteworthy is the way the aircraft has been patched up, with a swastika marking each bullet hole. Barely visible is the '1' repeated in white on the upper port wing, the number on the tail being black on a yellow disc. Bouvarre was credited with three victories (all shared) during the campaign (*via Author*)

D.520 were still in the making. The Morane would soon be relegated to playing a supporting role.

Heir to the famous 'Stork' fighter units of World War 1, GC I/2 was one of the units based 'where nothing happened' at Beauvais-Tillé, an airfield 75 km (47 miles) north of Paris – too far away from the frontline. When the unit's pilots landed there a few days before the declaration of war, they were greeted by villagers who had suffered heavily during the previous conflict. 'Look! Our storks are back', exclaimed the crowd that had gathered to welcome GC 1/2. M Barbier, a farmer whose fields were next to the aerodrome, came to see the 1st *Escadrille's* CO, Cne Robert Williame, to ask if he would agree to his daughters being the patrons of his squadron. In a simple and moving ceremony seven Moranes were christened with the names of the seven Barbier daughters, Williame choosing the youngest, Juliette.

It was not until seven months later that GC I/2 saw its first combat, on 2 April 1940. One Morane and one Messerschmitt were damaged. The unit was less fortunate the following day, however. Getting too close to his quarry in order to bring his guns to bear, Adj Henri Bruckert was hit by the return fire from a Do 17 of 4.(F)/121. He tried to land at Erstein, but, blinded by the heavy black smoke pouring out of his engine, he struck a tree he had not seen. The Morane exploded, killing Bruckert instantly.

A few minutes later the sections from GC I/2 and GC II/3 that had been unable to catch the fleeing Dornier ran into a gaggle of nine Bf 110s from V.(Z)/LG 1 that were escorting another Do 17. Adj Jean Le Martelot dived after the enemy fighters, his two wingmen close behind him. Opening fire on two Bf 110s from 100 m down to 50 m (110 yds to 55 yds), the French pilots saw one of their targets fall away in flames.

A third Bf 110, flown by future *Zerstörer* ace Leutnant Werner Methfessel, then attacked Le Martelot, wounding him in his left arm. When blood splashed over his face Le Martelot made a clumsy attempt

Pilots of the 1st *Escadrille* of GC I/2 with the seven Barbier sisters in their Sunday best at Beauvais-Tillé in late August 1939. Second from left is Cne Robert Williame, the *escadrille* commander, with Juliette, and standing in the middle is Adj Bruckert (with Mercedes), who was killed in action on 2 April 1940 (*via Author*)

to wipe it away, but he only succeeded in inadvertently ripping off his oxygen mask and losing consciousness. When he regained his senses he saw that his Morane was at an altitude of 800 m (2625 ft) and climbing steadily. Although Le Martelot made it to Lunéville, his badly mauled aircraft flipped onto its back on landing. People ran to help him out of the cockpit, but when they suddenly dropped the Morane's tail it triggered the machine guns, killing a nurse, four soldiers and two children.

The campaign was over for Le Martelot, but not the war. After a long recovery period he volunteered to join the *Groupe Normandie* on the Russian Front, where he claimed a Junkers Ju 87 in August 1944.

On 7 April 12 MS.406s of GC II/7 and four from GC I/6 spotted a lone Junkers Ju 52/3m transport belonging to *Fl.Komp.Ln.Regt.ObdL* that was reportedly flying a radio intercept mission in low and heavy clouds. This sitting duck made an awesome flying target, and almost all of the Morane pilots had a run at it as if they were on a firing range. No fewer than 11 pilots submitted claims. However, the staff of the *Zone d'Opérations Aériennes Sud* (ZOAS, Air Operations Area South) were less generous and awarded a kill to only three of them, all from GC II/7 – Cne Marie Papin-Labazordière, Sous-Lt Henri Jeandet and Sgt-chef Jean Doudiès. The latter had already been credited with a Do 17 on 2 March, and he would add another victory with the Morane, two with the Dewoitine and two flying Spitfires. Doudiès was reported missing off the French Riviera on 8 August 1944.

Jeandet flew with GC II/7 until November 1947, when he was the unit's CO – he claimed a total of two victories with Moranes and six with Spitfires. Jeandet was killed in an aerial collision in October 1950.

The MS.406 would encounter enemy aircraft three more times before the Phoney War came to an end, on 8 April and 8 and 9 May. The last of these actions saw five aircraft of GC III/7 try in vain to bring down a Do 17 – Polish pilot Lt Wladyslaw Goettel from GC II/7 had force-landed his MS.406 48 hours earlier after it had been bit by return fire from an He 111. Thus ended the nine-month period of 'no war nor peace'. 10 May 1940 was to mark the start of a war that would be anything but 'phoney'.

Between September 1939 and April 1940 MS.406 pilots had claimed 27 German aircraft destroyed, of which 25 were officially confirmed. No pilot achieved ace status during this period, although a few 'fledgling eagles' notched up their first kill or kills at this time. The cost was rather high, with 18 Moranes being destroyed by the enemy, six pilots killed, one taken prisoner and six wounded.

During the Phoney War several units were activated or reactivated and equipped with the Morane, such as GC III/1, GC I/6 and GC I/7. The latter was shipped to Lebanon in March 1940. Although it missed the Battle of France, it would be involved in another conflict a year later.

On 7 December 1939 GC I/3, which had claimed five victories, was withdrawn to southern France to become the first unit to convert to the long-awaited Dewoitine D.520. It was back in the frontline on 11 May – the day after the German onslaught in the West – and the unit claimed 48 more victories with this highly efficient fighter. Sous-Lt Émile Thierry, who had scored twice on 22 November 1939, added three more kills with the D.520 during the Battle of France to become an ace.

THE BATTLE OF FRANCE

O n 10 May 1940 the German armies marched into Holland and Belgium and started the penetration through the Ardennes that would lead to their decisive breakthrough at Sedan four days later, and their subsequent sweep behind the Allied troops massed in Belgium.

On the eve of the first day of the battle the *Armée de l'Air* had at its disposal the following MS.406s in frontline units (the number of immediately serviceable machines is in brackets);

Zone d'Opérations Aériennes Nord (ZOAN)
GC III/1 30 (20)	Norrent-Fontes	Cdt Paoli
GC II/2 26 (22)	Laon-Chambry	Cdt Bertrou
GC III/2 34 (28)	Cambrai-Niergnies	Cdt Geille
GC III/3 28 (23)	Beauvais-Tillé	Cne Le Bideau

Zone d'Opérations Aériennes Est (ZOAE)
GC I/2 31 (27)	Toul-Ochey	Cdt Daru
GC II/6 34 (20)	Anglure-Vouarces	Cdt Fontanet
GC III/7 34 (23)	Vitry-le-François	Cdt Crémont

Zone d'Opérations Aériennes Sud (ZOAS)
GC III/6 36 (30)	Chissey-sur-Loue	Cdt Castanier
GC II/7 35 (24)	Luxeuil-Saint-Sauveur	Cdt Durieux

Zone d'Opérations Aériennes Alpes (ZOAA)
GC I/6 25 (22)	Marseille-Marignane	Cdt Tricaud

On 10 May the Luftwaffe tried to pull off a major coup by attacking the main French airfields at dawn. This proved to be unsuccessful in the main, for despite German propaganda announcing triumphant results for the attacking bombers, few aircraft were actually destroyed on the ground. Indeed, most of the Allied fighter force remained unscathed. GC III/2, however, suffered heavy losses at Cambrai, with six Moranes being destroyed. Nevertheless, the unit was quickly given the opportunity to strike back when, just after dawn, two German bombers flew over the airfield. Adj Antoine Moret opened fire on a He 111, but failed to score any hits;

'At this very moment, the second Heinkel flies past me for another bombing run over the airfield. I decide to chase it. Both Heinkels join each other and head east. I open fire on the right wingman from a three-quarter angle and below. I come in as close as I can and give it one burst. The right engine catches fire and I can see a large tear in the right wing. The aeroplane enters a dive. I make a second attack, but only my left

Sgt Jacques de Puybusque claimed seven victories in May-June 1940 and in January 1941 he was transferred to Indochina, where he met his death in an accident six months later. He is wearing the enamel stork badge on his chest, which was a privilege given to pilots of the 1st *escadrille* of GC I/2 who claimed at least two victories – de Puybusque was the first pilot to be awarded the stork in World War 2 (*via Author*)

machine gun is still working. Short of ammunition, I can only follow the track of the aeroplane, which keeps on losing altitude and vanishes near the ground.'

This He 111 was the second of the seven victories credited to Moret in May-June 1940, the last three being claimed after GC III/2 had converted to the H-75A. Antoine Moret, born in 1912, was in the reserve when he was called up again on the eve of war. In February 1943, following the Allies' capture of Vichy French territories in North Africa, Moret joined Curtiss P-40-equipped GC II/5 *Lafayette* in Tunisia and later added an eighth victory (a Focke-Wulf Fw 190) to his tally. He was killed on a training flight in January 1946.

GC I/2 claimed two Heinkels early on the morning of 10 May 1940. Sgt Jacques de Puybusque, who shared in the destruction of one of them, wrote in his personal diary;

'Scrambled and made contact with two Heinkel 111s. First combat, and had no idea of how to go about it. I opted for attacks from a three-quarter angle in the sun. Making eight runs, I shot at an average distance of 250 m [270 yds]. Some confusion in my first deflection shots, with better aiming later. To be remembered – open fire at short range, stay cold-blooded, "polish" deflections.'

GC III/1 had a good start, downing seven He 111s (one shared with MB.152s of GC II/8) and one Ju 88, but one pilot was wounded in a crash landing after his engine was shot up by the rear gunner of a Heinkel. Among the victors were Sgt Kléber Doublet, who claimed the Ju 88 as the first of his six kills, and Adj Edgar Gagnaire. At least five He 111s of I. and III./ KG 27 did not return, but unfortunately one of GC III/1's victims was actually an RAF Bristol Blenheim IV of No 57 Sqn. Doublet's 'Ju 88' was in fact a He 111P of III./KG 27, the crew of which was taken prisoner.

Although considered one of the élite units of the *Armée de l'Air*, GC II/7 had seen little combat during the Phoney War from its base at Luxeuil in eastern France. This unit turned out to be a 'factory of generals', for many of its members eventually became 'full star' officers. However, on 10 May Luxeuil was targeted by He 111s, which destroyed nine Moranes on the ground. Several pilots managed to get into the air, and the *patrouille* led by Cne Henri Hugo caught a Heinkel on a photo-reconnaissance mission, as related by Sgt Pierre Boillot;

'Thanks to a magnificent manoeuvre ordered by our leader [Hugo], we were able to intercept this German aeroplane, which was flying faster and higher than us. It made the mistake of turning inside of us, which helped our leader to be in a good shooting position for a few seconds – enough time to hit one of its engines. The enemy aeroplane slowed down, allowing the two young men that we were [Boillot was 22] to finish it off. That was all our glory – finishing off an aeroplane that would have gone down anyway!'

Pierre Boillot, promoted to the rank of adjudant in June and then commissioned in 1943, did not claim any further victories in the Morane, but added one flying the D.520 in June 1940 and six more in Spitfires from October 1943 through to March 1945. He retired in June 1969 with the rank of colonel, and died in 1994.

It was traditional in the *Armée de l'Air* that airmen were billeted in comfortable private homes near to their airfield. When the alarm was

given at Vauclerc (Vitry-le-François) of an incoming air raid, none of GC III/7's pilots were on site. Four Do 17s dropped their bombs and destroyed three MS.406s. However, a few pilots did show up in time to take off and chase the stragglers. Among them was Cdt Maurice Arnoux. At 45, he had re-enlisted to serve his country for what he called a '*baroud d'honneur*' (last-ditch struggle). This veteran, having achieved eight victories in World War 1 and been highly decorated for his successes, had won worldwide renown in the inter-war years as a racing pilot. However, his first operational mission did not live up to his expectations, as he ended it upside down.

When dusk fell on the first day of the 'real war' in the West, MS.406 units had fared much better than had been feared. They had claimed 21 confirmed victories (probables were not taken into account in this study), but had only lost eight aircraft in aerial combat, with three pilots being killed and two severely injured. Of course, the MS.406's well-known defects had not improved. Guns kept jamming above 4000 m (13,000 ft), and engines were still overheating when pilots tried to catch the fast German bombers, but morale was still high among the pilots.

Cdt Maurice Arnoux turned MS.406 Nº813 upside down upon landing after his first sortie on 10 May 1940. This *escadrille* had chosen Michelangelo's 'Fury' head as its insignia – a superb piece of artwork. The individual number '6' was repeated in white on the port wing. The star in a crescent above the unit insignia was probably a personal marking (*via Author*)

One such individual was Pierre Boillot, whose encounter with He 111s had left a lasting impression on him;

'We met Heinkel 111s on 10 May. They were fast – almost as fast as our poor Moranes – and to get at them took a lot of time if we did not attack them from higher up, which we seldom did because of the low performance of our early-warning system. In fact, we were usually warned of incoming air raids when bombs fell on our airfields. The first firing pass was to be made at point-blank range because you had few chances to make a second one. But, unlike the Dorniers we had met until then, the Heinkels could absorb much punishment, and wiping them out of the sky was a tedious and dangerous task.'

The worst was yet to come, however. The deadly Bf 109 was nowhere to be seen on 10 May, but it would soon make its mark on the campaign.

As it is not possible to review all of the aerial combats involving the MS.406 during the Battle of France in a volume of this size, we will deal only with the most significant events.

On 11 May at around 0930 hrs GC III/6 caught a formation of 16 He 111s of I./KG 51 over Besançon. A straggler was singled out and shot down by seven pilots (plus one from GC II/7), including Adj-chef Pierre Le Gloan. Another Heinkel, belonging to III./KG 55, was credited to GC III/6 later in the day.

Based at Chissey, in the east of France, GC III/6 was too far away from the focal point of the land battle and could only intercept incoming bombers targeting cities and airfields in southern France, such as Dijon, Lyons and even Marseille. Until the unit was sent to Coulommiers, near Paris, on 20 May, it would see only reduced activity.

An He 111 of 9./KG 51 claimed by GC II/7 near Avallon on 11 May was credited to 16 pilots – a record! They included Cne Henri Hugo and Sous-Lt Georges Valentin. During the first two days of the campaign GC II/7 registered four confirmed victories but lost two pilots killed and two injured, plus 18 Moranes lost to all causes, including 12 destroyed on the ground by the Luftwaffe.

Sgt-chef Adonis Moulèmes and Sgt Charles Boyer of GC III/7 took off to intercept a large formation of He 111s of KG 53 striking Saint-Dizier and Toul during the morning of 11 May, Moulèmes later reporting;

'As I warn my wingman about the enemy bombers, two Heinkel 111s fly below us in close formation. One of them shoots at my wingman. I immediately go on the attack, but my first pass from three-quarter astern misses. On the third one I break off underneath and see its undercarriage lowered. After three more passes made from three-quarter front, the right engine stops and it flies on one wing, in a nose-up attitude. During each of my passes it fires back and loses height. In five minutes it is down from 2000 m to 900 m [6500 ft to 2950 ft]. At 0638 hrs I lose sight of the Heinkel 111, but at the same moment I can see black smoke rising to a height of 300 m [1000 ft] from a wooded hill.'

Carried away by his momentum and his enthusiasm, Boyer had hit the tail of another bomber with his wing. He managed to return to base, where he thought it more prudent to conceal the collision from his commanding officer.

Adonis Moulèmes was one of the three pilots from GC III/7 who flew to England on the last day of the battle (the other two being Albert Littolff and André Feuillerat). He enlisted in the Free French Air Force and was taken prisoner by the Vichy French at Dakar in September 1940. Sentenced to death for desertion, he was subsequently pardoned but was only released from jail in 1944. He scored twice during May-June 1940.

Early in the morning of 12 May GC III/1 intercepted a lone He 111 on a reconnaissance mission over Belgium. No fewer than 11 Moranes made several passes at it, riddling the fuselage and wings with bullets and stopping both engines. The Heinkel, belonging to *Stab* KG 54, crashed into the Escaut River and its crew were made PoWs. As was the custom in the *Armée de l'Air*, each of the 11 pilots who took part in the destruction of the enemy aircraft was awarded a full victory (see Appendix 2). This sortie underlines the challenge that these big bombers presented to the underarmed Moranes.

Later in the day a patrol clashed with Bf 110s of III./ZG 26 south of Antwerp. One was claimed, but GC III/1 lost three Moranes, two pilots being injured. For Adj Pierre Déchanet (probably shot down by Leutnant Sophus Baagoe, a future *Zerstörer* ace) the campaign was over, but not the war. He resumed fighting with the *Normandie-Niémen* on the Russian Front in January 1944 and added five more victories at the controls of Yakovlev fighters to the one he had claimed on 10 May 1940.

Many Polish fighter pilots had fled to France after their country fell into German hands. Following training to *Armée de l'Air* standards and basic tuition in French, six *patrouilles* of three pilots each (plus three mechanics, one rigger, three mechanical assistants and three soldiers) were assigned to GC III/1, GC I/2, GC III/2, GC III/6 and GC II/7 on 27 March. One of the pilots, Lt Jozef Brzezinski of the 1st *Escadrille* of GC I/2, possessed a special skill. He could hear incoming air raids before the lookouts sounded the alarm, as his *escadrille* commander, Cne Robert Williame, wrote in his memoirs;

'I found Brzezinski in the midst of his officers and NCOs. I had just given my orders regarding his "troika" when I witnessed the "Brzezinki mimic". He raised his right forefinger and said, "Ui, ui . . . ou, ouou, ouou!" Then he slapped his right forearm with his left hand in a gesture which in every country of the world means that it is time to run.'

Fortunately, the German bombers missed GC I/2 at Toul-Ochey on 12 May, but the unit would not always be so lucky.

By 13 May GC II/2 had only added three more victories (and twice as many probables) to its two kills from the Phoney War, thus exemplifying

MS.406s of GC III/6 lined up at Wez-Thuisy on 27 March 1940 with, third in the row, Cne Mieczyslaw Sulerzycki's aircraft sporting the Polish national red-and-white chequerboard on its fuselage. Sulerzycki was one of the 136 Poles incorporated into French fighter units. His own *patrouille* carried out 60 sorties and claimed two victories. Surviving Poles were evacuated to Great Britain, mostly via Gibraltar, on 22 June 1940. Many successfully took part in the Battle of Britain (*SHD/Air*)

A line-up of MS.406s at Lyon-Bron on 27 March 1940. The first ten *patrouilles* are ready to join their operational units. Lyon-Bron was where all Polish airmen were trained. In the foreground is N°1031 allocated to Lt Kazimierz Bursztyn who was earmarked for GC III/1, and just behind is N°948, flown by Sous-Lt Wladislaw Chciuk, who fought with GC I/2 (*via Author*)

the great difficulties Morane pilots were experiencing in finishing off their prey. Dawn on the 13th found GC II/2 waiting on its airfield at Laon-Chambry for a Potez 63.11 to show up. However, at 0945 hrs instead of the French reconnaissance aircraft, five Do 17s of II./KG 76 appeared overhead, escorted by four Bf 110s of 6./ZG 76. Immediately, 12 Moranes led by their CO, Cdt Paul Bertrou, scrambled. The fight proved both bitter and cruel.

The French claimed two Bf 110s destroyed, but lost three pilots, and several other Moranes returned with substantial damage. Among those killed were Cne Henri de Gail, deputy commander, and Paul Bertrou. For many years it was thought that the latter collided with a Bf 110, but it now appears that he was shot down by Oberleutnant Heinz Nacke, a future *Ritterkreuzträger*. The wreckage of his aircraft was not found until April 1941.

In the early days of the German offensive GC III/2 was very active over Belgium and northern France, claiming seven confirmed victories to add to the Hs 126 the unit had shot down on 30 October 1939. On 13 May a GC III/2 *patrouille* fell upon a lone Hs 126 of 9.(H)/LG 2. The Morane pilots claimed it destroyed, as did their compatriots from D.520-equipped GC II/3, who arrived on the scene later. Although the observer was ejected and killed during the engagement, the Henschel did in fact return to its base.

One of the pilots from GC III/2 who was credited with this 'kill' was Cne Édouard Corniglion-Molinier. Although he did not attain 'acedom', his career was quite outstanding nevertheless. Born in 1898, he became a fighter pilot in World War 1 after disguising his date of birth. During the 1930s Corniglion-Molinier flew in the Spainish Civil War with Malraux on the Republican side. In the May-June 1940 campaign he claimed four victories (two shared) at 42 years of age. In March 1941 Corniglion-Molinier joined the Free French, and took command of the *Forces Aériennes Françaises Libres* (FAFL) in the Middle East in June 1942 and in Great Britain five months later. Flying several times on missions over Germany, Corniglion-Molinier ended the war with the rank of *général de brigade aérienne*, as the commanding officer of the *Forces Françaises de l'Atlantique*. He was several times a minister in the 1950s, and even Minister of Justice. He died in 1963.

At 0845 hrs on 13 May one *patrouille triple légère* of GC III/3 took off to protect Rozendaal, in the Netherlands. Forty-five minutes later the Moranes engaged a formation of He 111s, claiming one shot down. At 1000 hrs they spotted 18 Bf 109s of 1./JG 26 flying under the clouds. The French pilots initially dived for the ground before climbing up to attack the Germans from below and astern. This bold manoeuvre caught their opponents off guard, and in a matter of seconds two Bf 109s were brought down by Adj-chef René Roger. The Messerschmitt pilots soon fought back and the combat split up into individual dogfights. Two more Bf 109s were claimed, by Sgts Édouard Le Nigen and Marcel Jeannaud. The latter had already taken part in the destruction of two He 111s, and he would add a fourth victory on 20 May and a fifth one (a Consolidated Catalina off Oran) two years later. As for Le Nigen, more will be revealed about him later. GC III/3 lost Cne R Trouillard, CO of the 5th *Escadrille*.

The then Col Édouard Corniglion-Molinier (second from right) congratulates new American recipients of the Silver Star at Chelverston, home of the 305th Bombardment Group, on 25 July 1943. He himself flew several missions as a Boeing B-17 waist gunner over Germany (*US NARA*)

As it had been unable to make good the massive losses suffered by GC II/7 on 10 and 11 May, which added to those inflicted on other *Groupes*, the headquarters of the *Armée de l'Air* decided to convert this unit to the D.520 ahead of schedule.

GC II/2 lost another pilot on 14 May to add to the three aviators that had perished the day before. Lt Henri de Rohan-Chabot, who intercepted 15 Do 17s on his own, was shot down in flames almost certainly by the bombers' rear gunners. He was the fifth pilot from the *Groupe* to be killed since 10 May.

That same morning GC III/7 had only 13 serviceable aeroplanes left on strength. Nevertheless, between 1254 hrs and 1325 hrs, seven Moranes in three *patrouilles* claimed four Hs 126s (nicknamed 'snouts' by the French). Two were shared by four pilots and the other two by seven. Adj Albert Littolff was involved in each combat, and he increased his tally to five kills – he would add another Hs 126 in late June.

Fourth from the right, Édouard Le Nigen poses with pilots and mechanics of GC III/3. At far right is Lt Roger Trouillard, CO of the 5th *Escadrille*, who was killed on 13 May 1940 – he had claimed two victories prior to his death. Trouillard's name meant 'coward' in French, so he had an inscription painted on his Morane saying 'I only lose my bottle by name'! (*via Author*)

At 1100 hrs on 15 May GC II/6, which had been reinforced by the 6th *Escadrille* of GC III/3 since 11 May, was forced to evacuate Maubeuge-Élesmes as the German vanguard approached the airfield. Twenty-four of the 28 Moranes that took off landed at Le Quesnoy. En route, two *patrouilles* intercepted Do 17s of I./KG 76. Sgt Pierre de Brémond d'Ars shot down one of

Three leading figures of the early Free French Air Force. From left to right, Sous-Lt Albert Littolff, Cne Jean Tulasne and Sous-Lt James Denis, serving with *Groupe de Chasse* No 1 *Alsace* at Fuka in May 1942. Both Littolff and Tulasne would meet their death with *Normandie* on the Russian Front on 16 and 17 July 1943, respectively. Denis, the man who reportedly shot down Hans-Joachim Marseille, claimed nine victories and survived the war (*SHD/Air*)

them but, hit in return, he had to bail out – this proved to be his third, and last, victory. The GC II/6 CO, Cdt Raymond Fontanet, was also shot up and landed at Reims. Two other Moranes were destroyed in this combat.

Returning from a mission at about 0800 hrs, GC III/7 was ordered to intercept Do 17s of I./KG 2 over Sainte-Menehould. While Adj Littolff manoeuvred his *patrouille* into battle formation, the Do 17s suddenly changed course. Without waiting for orders, Lt René Challe dived on the bombers, followed by his two wingmen. His aircraft was instantly hit by a German gunner, which caused a glycol leak, but he kept on firing and shot up the port engine of the nearest Dornier, which rolled over and quickly lost altitude. However, Challe was hit in the chest by a bullet. When the glycol ignited he was compelled to bail out. Challe had suffered a punctured lung, which meant that his campaign was over, but not his war. Indeed, together with one of his elder brothers, Maurice, he joined *Groupe Normandie* in Russia in March 1944. Wounded again in January 1945, Challe had by then bagged eight kills in all.

Challe's was the only victory of the day for GC III/7, which mourned the loss of two pilots killed and two severely injured.

On a 16 May reconnaissance flight over Montcornet two MS.406s of GC II/6 were shot down by flak, both pilots being wounded, but worse was to come. At 1215 hrs 18 Do 17s bombed Le Quesnoy in groups of six. The weak anti-aircraft defences were both slow to respond and inaccurate, letting the Dornier crews take their time to comb through the airfield. No fewer than 18 Moranes were destroyed, leaving only four of GC II/6's machines and one belonging to the 6ᵉ *Escadrille* of GC III/3 intact. Luckily, only one man, a Polish mechanic, was killed.

Unable to carry out any further missions, and with the enemy just 15 km away from the airfield, Cdt Fontanet decided on his own initiative

On 16 May GC III/2 was badly hit at Vertain, with no fewer than 18 of its Moranes being written off. These two aircraft of the 3rd *Escadrille*, N°688 and N°78, were left behind when the *Groupe* fell back to Beauvais the next day (*ECPA-D*)

to fall back to Beauvais the next day. As there were not enough MS.406s available to re-equip the *Groupe*, Headquarters sent GC II/6 to Châteauroux-Déols for conversion to the MB.152. With three victories, Sgt Pierre de Brémond d'Ars was GC II/6's most successful Morane pilot.

During the morning of 18 May a single *patrouille* from GC III/2 was looking for German bombers in the vicinity of Saint-Quentin when it was bounced by Bf 109s of I./JG 76. Leutnant Anton Stangl

shot down two Moranes, killing Lt Jacques Peuto and seriously wounding Sgt François Vittini. Another *patrouille*, acting as top cover, dived on the Messerschmitts, and Sgt-chef Georges Elmlinger damaged one, which was forced to crash land.

Georges Elmlinger, aged 24, was wounded on 9 June. During the campaign he was credited with six victories – five with the MS.406 (all shared except one) and one with the H-75A. Transferred to GC III/6, he shot down a Gloster Gladiator during the fighting in Syria in June 1941, and then joined GC III/3, with which he gained a last victory – a Fleet Air Arm Fairey Albacore – on 8 November 1942.

GC I/6 had been recreated at Marseille-Marignane on 15 December 1939, and the unit was still there at the time of the German onslaught. It was not until 17 May that the unit was included in the Order of Battle of *Groupement de Chasse* No 23 on its new airfield at Lognes-Émerainville, near Paris. It flew its first sorties on the following day, and this proved to be to be an inauspicious start.

At 1330 hrs a *patrouille triple* engaged Do 17s and Bf 110s. Cne Mauvier, CO of the 1st *Escadrille*, was hit by return fire and bailed out over enemy lines. At 1900 hrs, after another encounter with Do 17s, one *patrouille* was singled out by a German anti-aircraft battery. The Morane flown by Cne Bruneau, commanding officer of the 2nd *Escadrille*, was set on fire and he deliberately crashed onto the battery, allowing his wingmen to escape an unfortunate fate, although they were wounded and their

Sgt Pierre de Brémond d'Ars leans on MS.406 N°90 (his commander's aircraft) of GC II/6's 3rd *Escadrille* at Anglure-Vouarces in the autumn of 1939 – Léon Cuffaut can be seen standing by the same aircraft on page 13 (*SHD/Air*)

German soldiers inspect MS.406 N°605 of GC III/2, abandoned at Cambrai-Niergnies. Note the 5th *Escadrille* badge behind the cockpit – a black griffon on a red disc. Sous-Lt André Lansoy was at the controls of this machine on 17 May when he attempted to take off amid the bombs whilst Cambrai-Niergnies was under attack, but it suffered blast damage, forcing the pilot to abort his mission. Lansoy was credited with four victories in May-June 1940 (*ECPA-D*)

aircraft severely damaged. Deprived of its two *escadrille* leaders, and with its strength reduced to 12 of the 23 MS.406s that had been available in the morning, GC I/6 was left to rest for two days.

This *Groupe* would hold the sad record for the highest number of pilots put out of commission during the campaign – ten killed, three captured and nine seriously injured, for 13 confirmed victories. It lost four *commandants d'escadrille*. The primary reason for this mortifying rate of attrition was that from 5 June onwards GC I/6 primarily flew strafing missions.

Late in the afternoon of 19 May one *patrouille triple* of GC III/1 and one *patrouille double* of GC II/2 intercepted Bf 109s of I.(J)/LG 2 near Guise. Although the French pilots engaged the Messerschmitts with the dual advantages of surprise and height, the combat quickly became one-sided. While GC III/1 claimed only three probables, GC II/2 was credited with one confirmed and three probables. Their opponents, I.(J)/LG 2, lost the Bf 109 flown by future *Ritterkreuzträger* Friedrich-Wilhelm Strakeljahn, who was captured. GC III/1 lost three aircraft, with one pilot being killed and another wounded, but GC II/2 was more fortunate. Lt Tony Leenhardt (who claimed three victories with GC III/1) reported the loss of Lt Paul Marche;

'We see several Me 109s [*sic*] either at our altitude or lower. Our patrol leaders waggle their wings and at the same time we all dive on the Me 109s. We engage in many dogfights, and I notice an Me 109 sitting on the tail of a Morane. I forget the Me 109 I was targeting to help the Morane. Coming high from the sun, I close in fast but, as I open fire, it does the same and breaks away in a dive. The Morane has been hit – it catches fire and rolls over slowly onto its back. I can see it now diving straight to the ground, engulfed in flames, and it crashes near a village I assume to be Anzy-le-Château. I do not believe the pilot has been able to take to the silk.'

Having taken part in the shooting down of an Hs 126 of 1.(H)/11, which, incidentally was polished off by Hurricanes of No 85 Sqn, RAF, Sgt Édouard Le Nigen of GC III/3 claimed another near Le Quesnoy (this loss has not been recorded in the German archives). At around 1830 hrs

Lt Tony Leenhardt of GC III/1 in front of MS.406 Nº439 early in the war. This aircraft belonged to the 2nd *Escadrille* of GC I/2 and wore the name *FLANDRE* beneath its cockpit – this *escadrille* used to christen its early Moranes with the names of French provinces. The fighter was lost when Sous Lt Le Martelot flipped it over on to its back while landing on 2 April 1940 (*via Author*)

GC III/3 brought down a lone Do 17P of 4.(F)/11 near Valenciennes, and on their way back to base the Moranes crossed the path of four Bf 109s belonging to 5./JG 2. Unteroffizier Hans-Joachim Hartwig's aircraft was shot at successively by Adj-chef René Roger, Le Nigen and Czech pilot Sgt Bedrish Kratkoruky. The Messerschmitt crashed near Courtrai and was credited to the three airmen.

At 0730 hrs the following day GC I/6 encountered Do 17s of I./KG 3 southeast of Amiens, and Sous-Lt Henri Raphenne claimed one of them (identified as a 'Ju 86'). Then the Moranes had to fight their way home after being engaged by Bf 109s of I./JG 1. Although three were claimed, only one was actually lost. However, these victories were again won at high cost, for two pilots were wounded and Raphenne destroyed his aircraft while making an emergency landing.

Later that same day (20 May) at around 1800 hrs, nine Moranes of GC I/2 tackled 30+ Bf 109s of I./JG 27 and I./JG 51 near Reims. Sgt Jacques de Puybusque, flying as number two to Cne Robert Williame, found himself right behind a Messerschmitt. He opened fire at close range and the enemy fighter exploded in mid-air. Williame also fired at a Bf 109, but he was in turn hit by several opponents. The Frenchman managed to shake the German fighters off his tail and return to Damblain. However, his aircraft was a write-off, having probably been shot up by Hauptmann Helmut Riegel, *Kommandeur* of I./JG 27. Riegel, who was subsequently killed in action on 20 July 1940, had designed the unit's famous emblem of the tiger head superimposed on a silhouette of Africa.

Puybusque's Messerschmitt (probably from 3./JG 51) was duly confirmed. He wrote in his diary;

'See many Messerschmitt 109s. Bad approach, we are topped off. I chase a M.109 [*sic*] off my capitaine's tail and follow another that I soon shoot down. To be remembered – attack the M.109s only by surprise or with an altitude advantage. Be very patient, shoot at 20 m [22 yds]. Results – 1 M.109 shot down, 1 Morane riddled with bullets. My total – 2.'

Following his second confirmed victory, in accordance with the traditions of the 'Stork' *Escadrille*, Puybusque was entitled to wear an enamel stork badge on his chest.

20 May also saw the last big engagement by MS.406s of GC III/3. At 1730 hrs a large formation of He 111s, protected by Bf 110s of III./ZG 26, approached the *Groupe's* airfield at Beauvais-Tillé. The German fighters bounced the Moranes just after they had taken off, creating much confusion among the French pilots. Sgt Edgar Le Nigen thought that he was being attacked by bombers, but he struck back;

'Those dirty bombers are lions. They had the cheek to come after me. Frightened among all the fireballs, I struggled like a mad man and I got two of them.'

Indeed, two Bf 110s were brought down at the cost of one Morane, the pilot of which escaped uninjured. Le Nigen had already bagged an He 111

France's ranking MS.406 ace, Sgt Édouard Le Nigen, with what looks like a war trophy. Having re-enlisted for one year as a pilot with GC III/3 in 1938, he was sent home two weeks before mobilisation. Le Nigen was soon reassigned to his previous unit, however (*SHD/Air*)

that morning, and his tally now stood at ten victories (six shared). He would claim two more kills (two Hs 126s shared, both on 16 June) flying the D.520. The blazing ace of GC III/3 was hospitalised on 25 July 1940 for appendicitis and he never regained consciousness after the operation. He was 24.

In mid-April GC III/3 had been earmarked to convert to the D.520, but the misfortunes of GC II/7 changed priorities. The first Dewoitine fighters were finally taken on to the strength of GC III/3 on 23 May. Temporarily sidelined, the *Groupe's* pilots would resume fighting with their new mounts from 3 June onwards.

On 21 May GC I/6 suffered a new misfortune when four Moranes chasing a Do 17 unexpectedly overflew Cambrai-Niergnies airfield, which was now the new home of I./JG 3. The French pilots suddenly spotted a Fieseler Fi 156 Storch of 3.(H)/21, which was intending to land at the airfield – wrong place, wrong time! Cne Marcel Silvestre de Sacy switched to this new target and shot it down in flames under the eyes of the German personnel on the airfield, whereupon Bf 109s were hurriedly scrambled and caught up with the Moranes, bringing down two and severely damaging two others. Silvestre de Sacy was killed, thus becoming the second 1st *Escadrille* CO to be lost, and *Groupe* CO Cdt Georges Tricaud bailed out and returned four days later.

Tricaud, aged 39, was part of the 'old guard', but unlike most of his counterparts, he did fight in the air alongside his pilots. He claimed three victories in 1940 and two more against Grumman F4F Wildcats of VF-41 over Casablanca on 8 November 1942. He met his death during this combat.

The last victory for GC III/7 with the MS.406 came on 21 May when a Bf 109 was credited to Sgt Louis Berthet (his third, and last). Prospects looked bleak for the *Groupe* when, at 1820 hrs, 15 of its Moranes engaged 50+ Bf 109s of III./JG 2 and II. and III./JG 53. Albert Littolff later wrote, 'Totally outnumbered, our sections were scattered from the beginning. Then, a succession of individual dogfights at one-to-ten'. Berthet was attacked from dead astern and a bullet broke one of his legs, but the Messerschmitt pilot made the mistake of overshooting and Berthet got hits in his opponent's engine. Heavily smoking, the Bf 109 entered a spin with no possible recovery. Five Moranes were lost, as well as two pilots.

Three days later it was GC II/7's turn to fight its last engagements with the Morane before converting to the D.520. Cnes Marie Papin-Labazordière and Henri Hugo brought down a He 111 of 8./KG 51 not far from the Haut-Koenigsbourg fortress.

Henri Hugo, 28 years old, was credited with six victories during the campaign, all bar one on the Morane, and all shared. He escaped from occupied France in May 1943 and took over GC 2/7 *Nice* (aka No 326 [French] Sqn), flying Spitfires, in September. He ended the war with the rank of commandant and as CO of the 4th *Escadre de Chasse* (Fighter Wing). Hugo retired as a full general in 1963 and died in 1996.

At 1500 hrs on 25 May a *patrouille triple* of GC III/1 took off to escort a Potez 63.11 reconnaissance aircraft between Arras and Cambrai. Adj Edgar Gagnaire, delayed by technical problems with his fighter, lagged behind the formation and elected to land at Le Plessis-Belleville. However, en route he encountered three Ju 52/3m transports returning from a mission;

'What a lucky strike! I chose the one that straggled behind and closed in from three-quarters and below. It had not seen me, so I took all my time to set it on fire. It rolled over and struck the ground in a matter of seconds. The next one had seen what had happened and tried to take evasive actions, to no avail. However, I only nailed it down after my third pass. It crashed close to the first one. I pulled up to 500 m [1650 ft] to deal with the third Junkers, but at that moment I observed another Junkers that was landing near the first one I had shot down to help its passengers. I made three firing passes at it and left it smoking.'

Oddly enough, Gagnaire was officially credited with two Ju 88s in the air and one 'liaison aircraft' on the ground. This pair of victories brought his grand total to five (he was one of the 11 victors over the He 111 on 12 May).

Things had gone from bad to worse for GC III/6. On the previous day (24 May) it had lost its CO, Cdt Pierre Castanier, whose fighter had been hit by Bf 110s of III./ZG 76. He was then mortally wounded by French anti-aircraft fire before he bailed out. Another pilot from the unit was taken prisoner. On 25 May five more MS.406s were written off, one pilot being killed and one injured. In the evening GC III/6 was left with only five serviceable aircraft.

Sous-Lt Pierre Le Gloan (right) with Sous-Lt Léon Cuffaut relax after an aerial combat exercise in Algiers in early 1941. Behind them is Le Gloan's D.520 N°277, wearing his lucky number '6' (*via Author*)

It was withdrawn on 31 May and sent to Le Luc, near Toulon in southern France, to rest and recuperate. The unit would soon convert to the D.520.

GC III/6's Adj-chef Pierre Le Gloan, aged 27, was a born fighter pilot, claiming four victories with the MS.406 and 14 with the D.520, including five Italian aircraft in one sortie on 15 June 1940. For his achievement he was commissioned on the spot. To this tally he added seven British fighters in Syria during June-July 1941. After the Vichy *Armée de l'Air* merged with the Free French to give way to the *Forces Aériennes Françaises* in July 1943, GC III/6 converted to the Bell P-39 Airacobra. On 11 September 1943 Pierre Le Gloan forgot to jettison his belly tank before attempting a forced landing brought about by engine trouble, and he was killed instantly when his Airacobra exploded upon touching the ground.

On 26 May 12 MS.406s of GC III/1 took off at 0730 hrs and joined up with five H-75As of GC I/4 to escort two Potez 63.11s on a reconnaissance sortie along the Péronne-Valenciennes axis. They tangled with Bf 109s of I./JG 21 near Péronne, Sgt Kléber Doublet claiming two of the enemy fighters destroyed, as did Adj-chef Roger Saussol. The latter did not escape the action unscathed, however, as he later recalled;

'We engaged in combat five kilometres southwest of Cambrai at 1500 m [4900 ft]. After having shot down two enemy fighters with four bursts of fire, I tried to get at a third one but found myself alone and being chased by five others. We briefly exchanged fire and they got away. I then headed south at low level. Five minutes later I saw a small German aircraft but I had run out of ammo. Then two German fighters showed up. After a long and exhausting dogfight my engine was hit and took fire. I barely avoided high-tension wires and finally belly-landed. I was taken prisoner. I had a bullet in my right calf and severe burns to my face and hands. I remained blind for three weeks.'

Saussol was released from custody in March 1941 to receive medical care in France. His personal record stood at five confirmed victories. As for Kléber Doublet, he claimed an Hs 126 of 4.(H)/21 (shared victory) a few minutes later, bringing his grand total to five.

Later that same day a heavy blow was suffered by GC III/1 when about 40 He 111s followed by 20 Do 17s strafed and bombed its airfield at Le Plessis-Belleville at 1330 hrs. No fewer than seven Moranes were completely destroyed, three more were damaged beyond repair and the runway was rendered useless by hundreds of bomb craters. Cdt Étienne Paoli, CO of GC III/1, flew into a rage when he realised that no anti-aircraft weapons had fired back because the gunners had run to shelters rather than man their guns. The *Groupe* had limited activity in the following days, pending the delivery of 'second-hand' Moranes that then needed to be overhauled because most of them were barely serviceable.

The airfield at Damblain was targeted the following day by four Bf 109s, probably from 7./JG 53, which strafed the Moranes of GC I/2 while the pilots of four more Messerschmitts watched the scene from above. Once again the alarm was given too late, with eight MS.406s being destroyed and another damaged beyond repair. For several days GC I/2 had to curtail its sorties.

On 29 May, having suffered many losses both on the ground (at least 16 Moranes were destroyed or damaged beyond repair at Cambrai-Niergnies) and in the air (three pilots killed and eight wounded), GC III/2 was ordered to Avord to convert to the H-75A.

Aircraft of GC II/2 and GC II/7 intercepted a Ju 88 of 4.(F)/121 on a photo-reconnaissance mission and shot it down northwest of Pontarlier on 1 June. As usual, a full victory was credited to each of the seven pilots who took part in the combat, including Adj-chef Pierre Dorcy;

'I had been on patrol for a few minutes when I saw a lone suspect aeroplane over Auxonne at around 4800 m [15,750 ft]. I headed towards him to cut off its route. I recognised a Heinkel 111 [*sic*]. We caught it in a pincer from astern at the same level and about 500 m [550 yds] behind. At the first pass the left engine quit. At the second, black smoke was

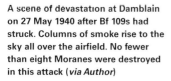

A scene of devastation at Damblain on 27 May 1940 after Bf 109s had struck. Columns of smoke rise to the sky all over the airfield. No fewer than eight Moranes were destroyed in this attack (*via Author*)

emitted from the right engine. The enemy slightly nosed down – we kept on firing. At about 10 km [six miles] from Pontarlier, Moranes or Dewoitines [D.520s in fact] appeared. I made a last pass from three-quarters ahead and below. The Heinkel was flying very low. It hit the ground once and disappeared behind trees.'

This was the fourth of the six victories claimed by Pierre Dorcy, all of them shared. He was then 32. Discharged in December 1942 when the *Armée de l'Air* ceased to exist, he joined the Resistance, was arrested by the *Gestapo* and deported to Germany in September 1944. Dorcy subsequently escaped to Switzerland and re-enlisted in the *Forces Aériennes Françaises* with the rank of sous-lieutenant.

On 2 June, after a 100 km [60-mile] full-throttle chase, a *patrouille double* of GC I/2 eventually caught up with 12 He 111s near Vesoul. Sgt Jacques de Puybusque was the first to open fire;

'Coming into contact with 11 He 111s, I report and, as my comrades seem to hesitate, I rush forward alone. Eager to show them that they must not fear to press home their attacks, I put into practice a tactic that looks to me to be very good – I make a three-quarter head-on pass, open fire at 50 m into the engine and break off as close as possible to the Hun. To be remembered – never break off above. Consequence – in flames, must bail out.'

The following day the Luftwaffe launched a large-scale offensive against the French airfields around Paris. This operation, codenamed *Unternehmen Paula* by the Germans, had been known of for some time by the French. Accordingly, they reinforced their defences and organised a counter-plan known as *Opération Tapir*. The alert was to be transmitted by the communications centre at the top of the Eiffel Tower. The scheme looked good on paper, but things went wrong on 3 June. Firstly, the Germans knew what the French were up to and effectively jammed the Eiffel Tower transmitter. Secondly, although the *Armée de l'Air* had supposedly reinforced its units around Paris, the coordination between the different *Groupements de Chasse* assigned to *Opération Tapir* left much to be desired, resulting in the fighter force being poorly controlled. However, if *Tapir* was a complete failure, *Paula* did not achieve its goal of smashing the French fighter force either.

At Lognes-Émerainville, GC I/6 was told to scramble at the last minute. One Morane was quickly shot down, but Sous-Lt Henri Raphenne challenged the faster Bf 109Es of II./JG 53 and brought down two of them, both pilots being killed. Again, GC I/6 bought its success at a high price – two pilots were killed and one seriously injured. Two of them probably fell victim to Adolf Galland.

After a long pause to eradicate the Dunkirk pocket, the Wehrmacht and the Luftwaffe launched the ultimate offensive against the French armies on 5 June that reached its climax 20 days later with an armistice. By then only five *Groupes de Chasse* were still flying the MS.406, and it was now too late to undertake their conversion. *(text continues on page 49)*

Looking like a caricature of a typical Frenchman as seen by foreigners, GC II/2's Adj-chef Pierre Dorcy, smoking a Gauloise and wearing a beret (he just lacks the baguette and the bottle of red wine), was, nevertheless, a tough warrior, claiming six victories. He joined the Resistance after the armistice and eventually the *Forces Aériennes Françaises* in late 1944 following his escape from a German camp (*SHD/Air*)

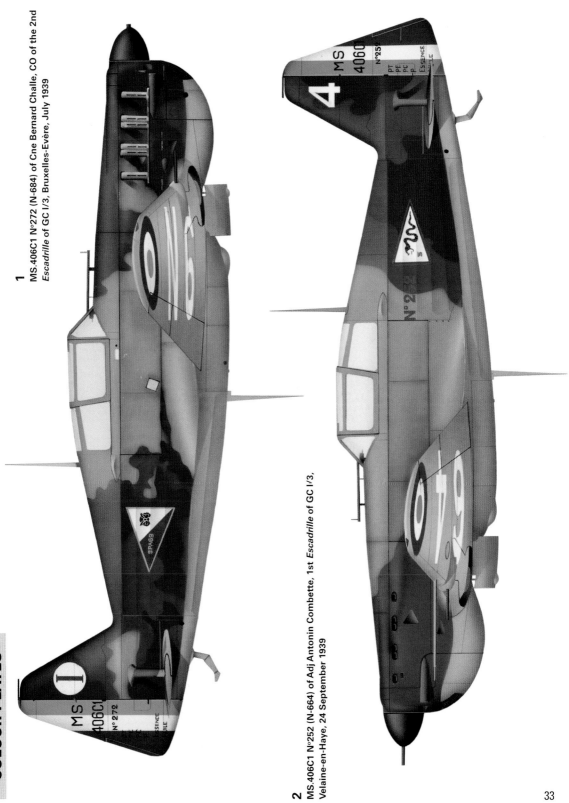

1
MS.406C1 N°272 (N-684) of Cne Bernard Challe, CO of the 2nd
Escadrille of GC I/3, Bruxelles-Evère, July 1939

2
MS.406C1 N°252 (N-664) of Adj Antonin Combette, 1st *Escadrille* of GC I/3,
Velaine-en-Haye, 24 September 1939

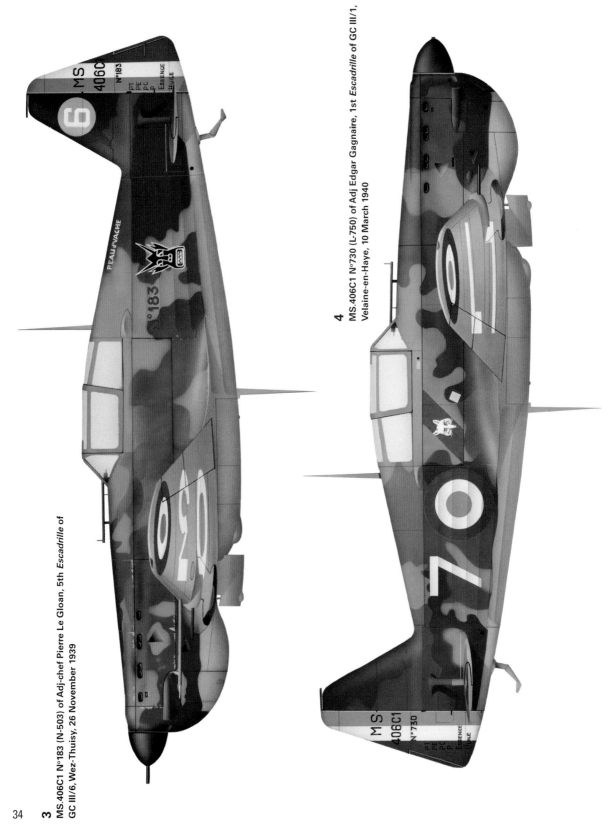

3
MS.406C1 N°183 (N-503) of Adj-chef Pierre Le Gloan, 5th *Escadrille* of
GC III/6, Wez-Thuisy, 26 November 1939

4
MS.406C1 N°730 (L-750) of Adj Edgar Gagnaire, 1st *Escadrille* of GC III/1,
Velaine-en-Haye, 10 March 1940

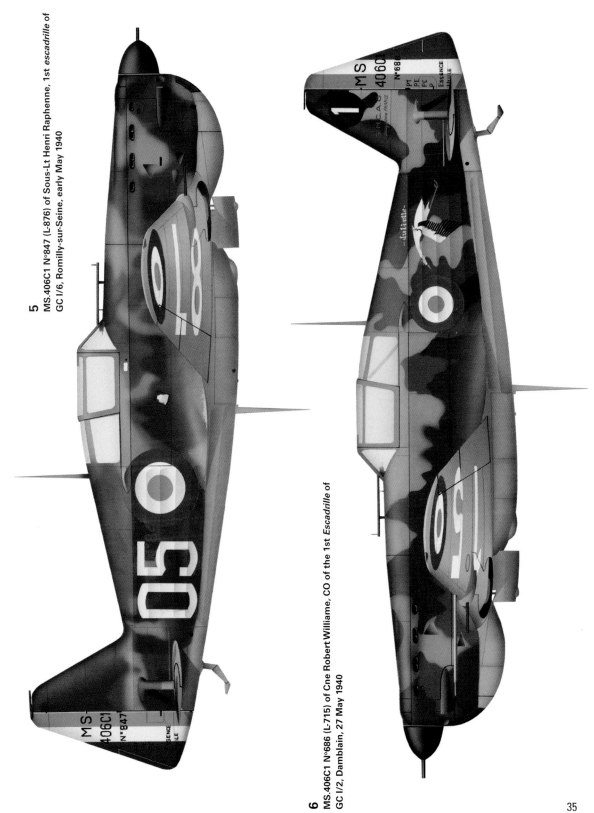

5
MS.406C1 N°847 (L-876) of Sous-Lt Henri Raphenne, 1st *escadrille* of
GC I/6, Romilly-sur-Seine, early May 1940

6
MS.406C1 N°686 (L-715) of Cne Robert Williame, CO of the 1st *Escadrille* of
GC I/2, Damblain, 27 May 1940

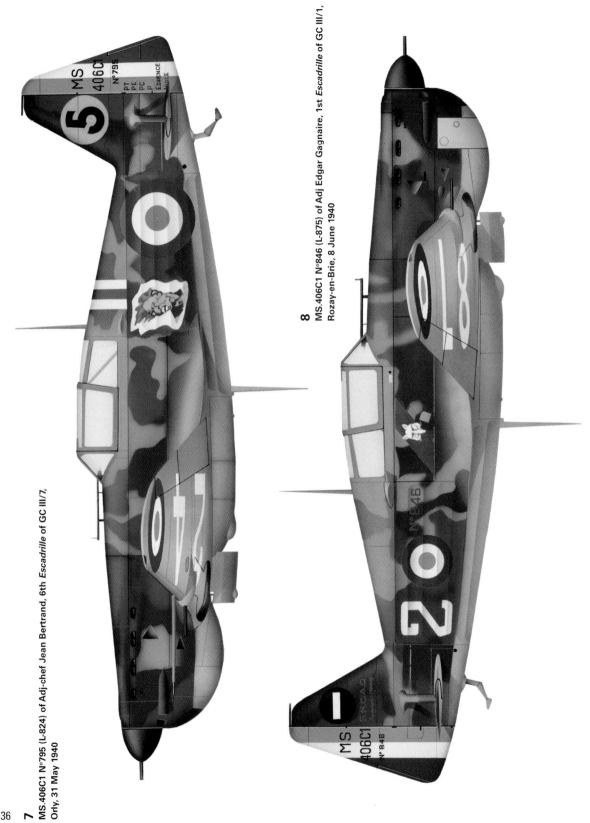

7
MS.406C1 N°795 (L-824) of Adj-chef Jean Bertrand, 6th *Escadrille* of GC III/7, Orly, 31 May 1940

8
MS.406C1 N°846 (L-875) of Adj Edgar Gagnaire, 1st *Escadrille* of GC III/1, Rozay-en-Brie, 8 June 1940

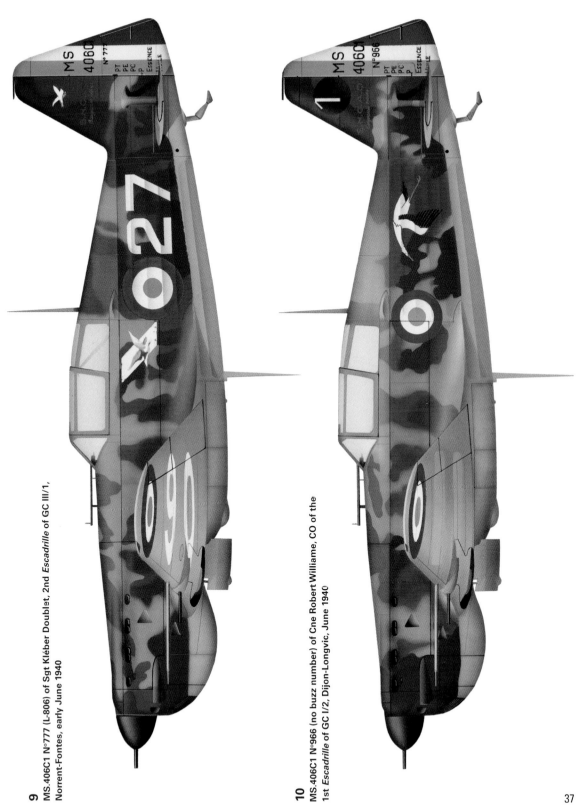

9
MS.406C1 N°777 (L-806) of Sgt Kléber Doublet, 2nd *Escadrille* of GC III/1,
Norrent-Fontes, early June 1940

10
MS.406C1 N°966 (no buzz number) of Cne Robert Williame, CO of the
1st *Escadrille* of GC I/2, Dijon-Longvic, June 1940

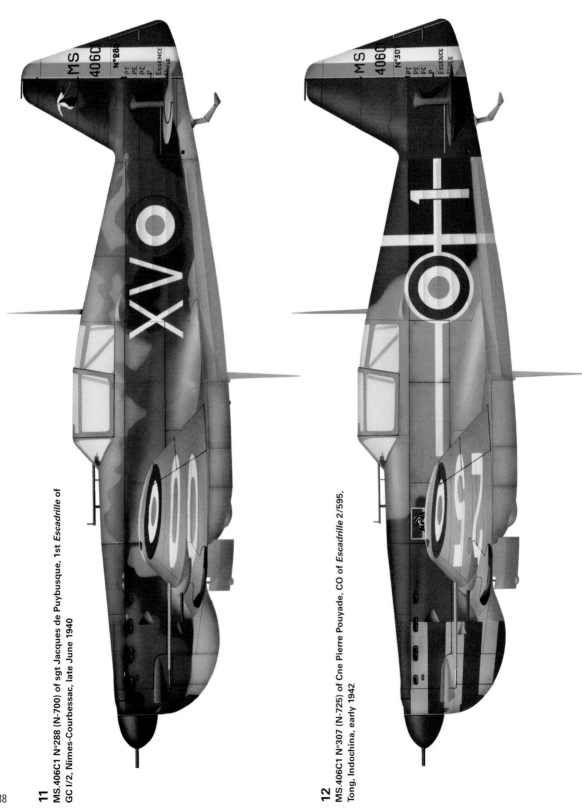

11
MS.406C1 N°288 (N-700) of sgt Jacques de Puybusque, 1st *Escadrille* of
GC I/2, Nimes-Courbessac, late June 1940

12
MS.406C1 N°307 (N-725) of Cne Pierre Pouyade, CO of *Escadrille* 2/595,
Tong, Indochina, early 1942

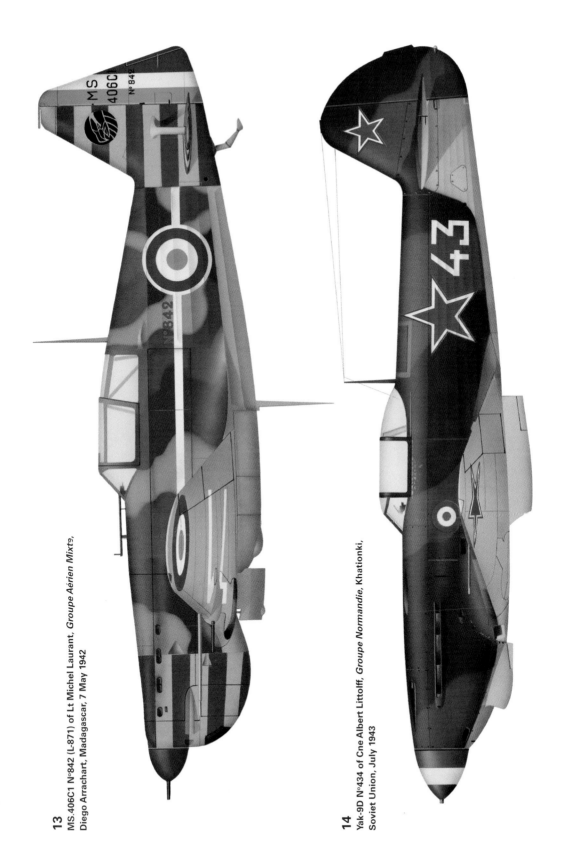

13
MS.406C1 N°842 (L-871) of Lt Michel Laurant, *Groupe Aérien Mixte*,
Diego Arrachart, Madagascar, 7 May 1942

14
Yak-9D N°434 of Cne Albert Littolff, *Groupe Normandie*, Khationki,
Soviet Union, July 1943

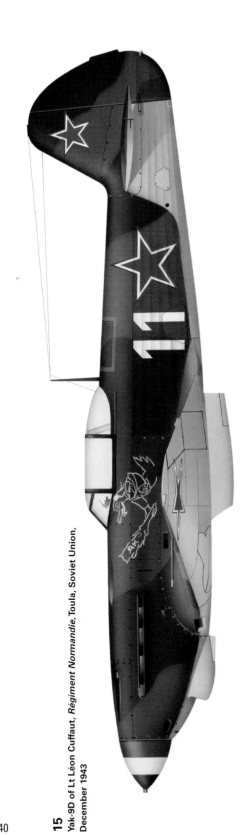

15
Yak-9D of Lt Léon Cuffaut, *Régiment Normandie*, Toula, Soviet Union,
December 1943

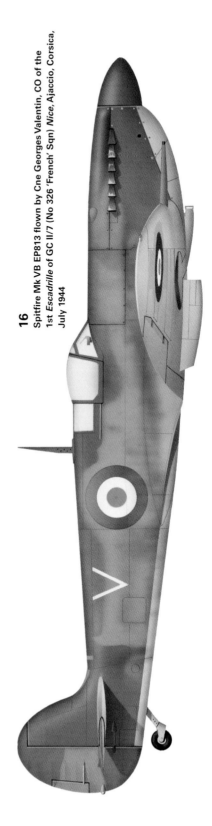

16
Spitfire Mk VB EP813 flown by Cne Georges Valentin, CO of the
1st *Escadrille* of GC II/7 (No 326 'French' Sqn) *Nice*, Ajaccio, Corsica,
July 1944

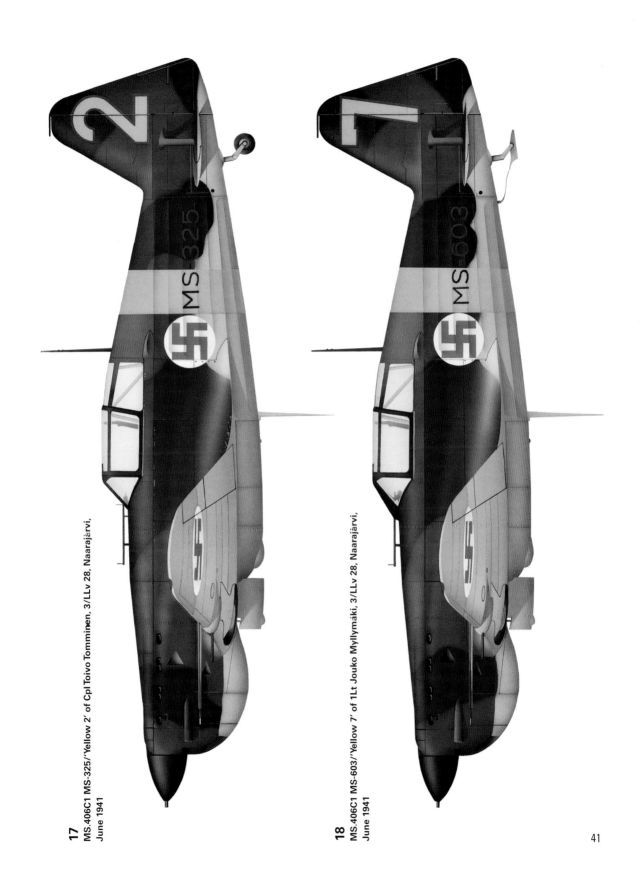

17
MS.406C1 MS-325/'Yellow 2' of Cpl Toivo Tomminen, 3/LLv 28, Naarajärvi,
June 1941

18
MS.406C1 MS-603/'Yellow 7' of 1Lt Jouko Myllymäki, 3/LLv 28, Naarajärvi,
June 1941

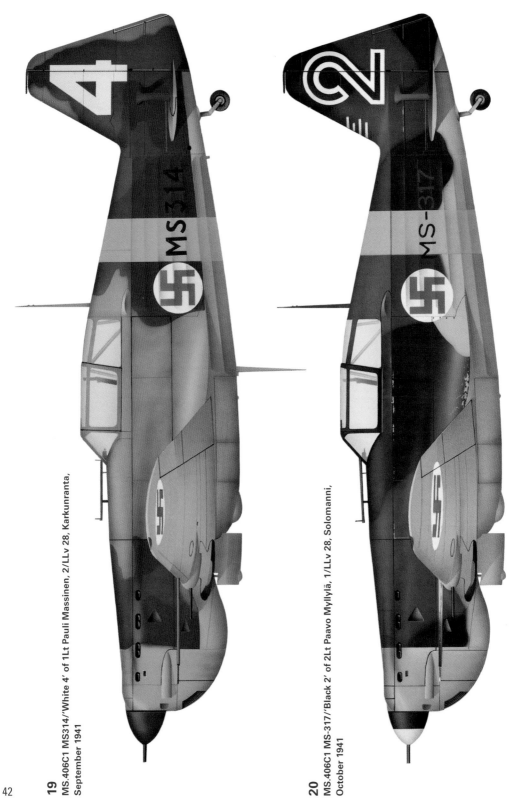

19
MS.406C1 MS314/'White 4' of 1Lt Pauli Massinen, 2/LLv 28, Karkunranta,
September 1941

20
MS.406C1 MS-317/'Black 2' of 2Lt Paavo Myllylä, 1/LLv 28, Solomanni,
October 1941

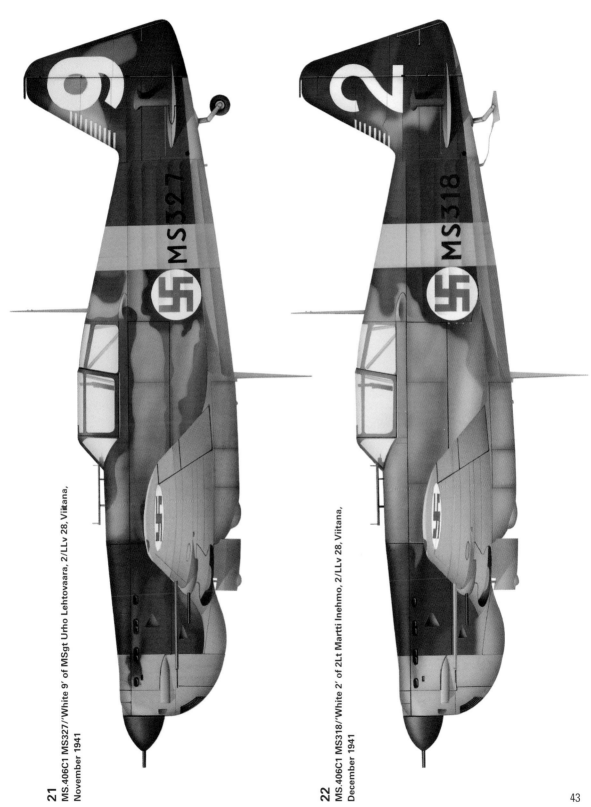

21
MS.406C1 MS327/'White 9' of MSgt Urho Lehtovaara, 2/LLv 28, Viitana,
November 1941

22
MS.406C1 MS318/'White 2' of 2Lt Martti Inehmo, 2/LLv 28, Viitana,
December 1941

43

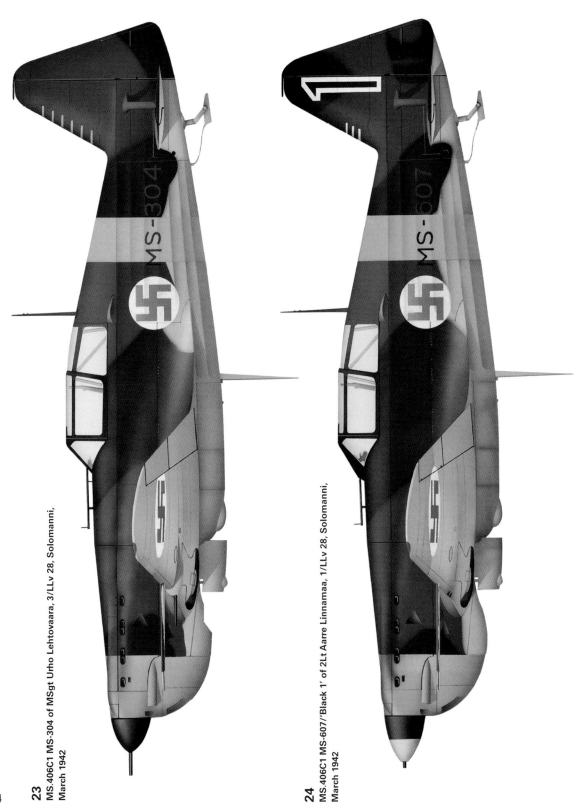

23
MS.406C1 MS-304 of MSgt Urho Lehtovaara, 3/LLv 28, Solomanni,
March 1942

24
MS.406C1 MS-607/'Black 1' of 2Lt Aarre Linnamaa, 1/LLv 28, Solomanni,
March 1942

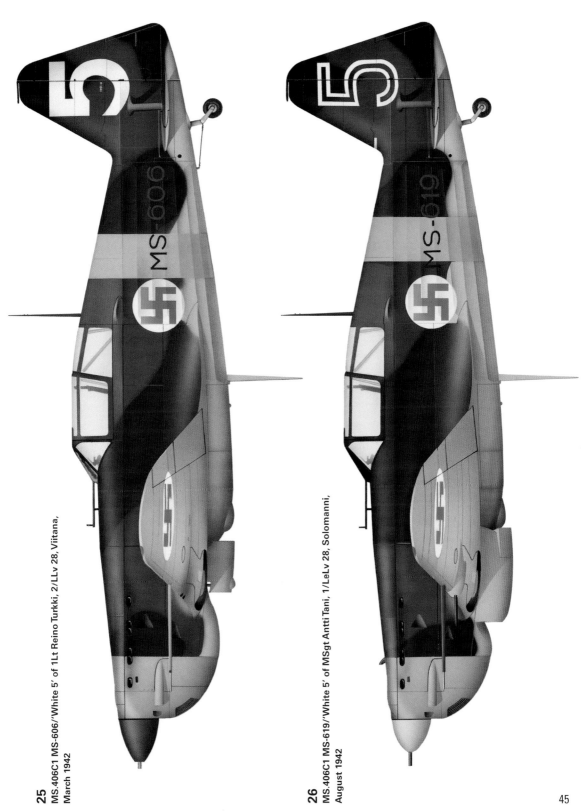

25
MS.406C1 MS-606/'White 5' of 1Lt Reino Turkki, 2/LLv 28, Viitana,
March 1942

26
MS.406C1 MS-619/'White 5' of MSgt Antti Tani, 1/LeLv 28, Solomanni,
August 1942

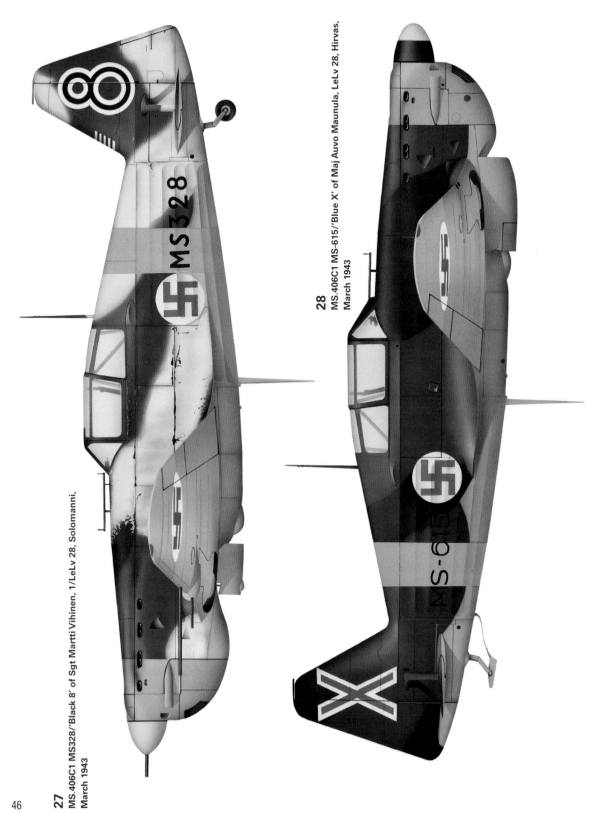

27
MS.406C1 MS328/'Black 8' of Sgt Martti Vihinen, 1/LeLv 28, Solomanni,
March 1943

28
MS.406C1 MS-615/'Blue X' of Maj Auvo Maunula, LeLv 28, Hirvas,
March 1943

46

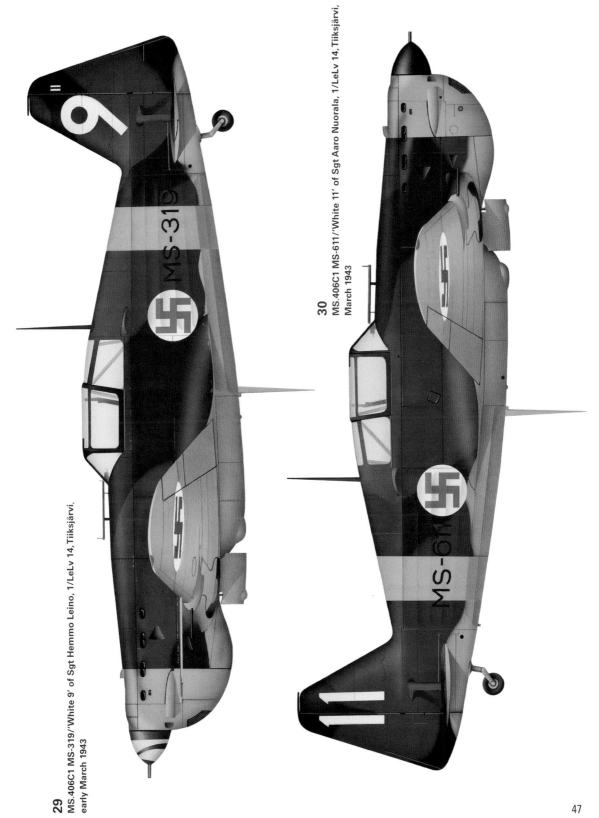

29
MS.406C1 MS-319/'White 9' of Sgt Hemmo Leino, 1/LeLv 14, Tiiksjärvi, early March 1943

30
MS.406C1 MS-611/'White 11' of Sgt Aaro Nuorala, 1/LeLv 14, Tiiksjärvi, March 1943

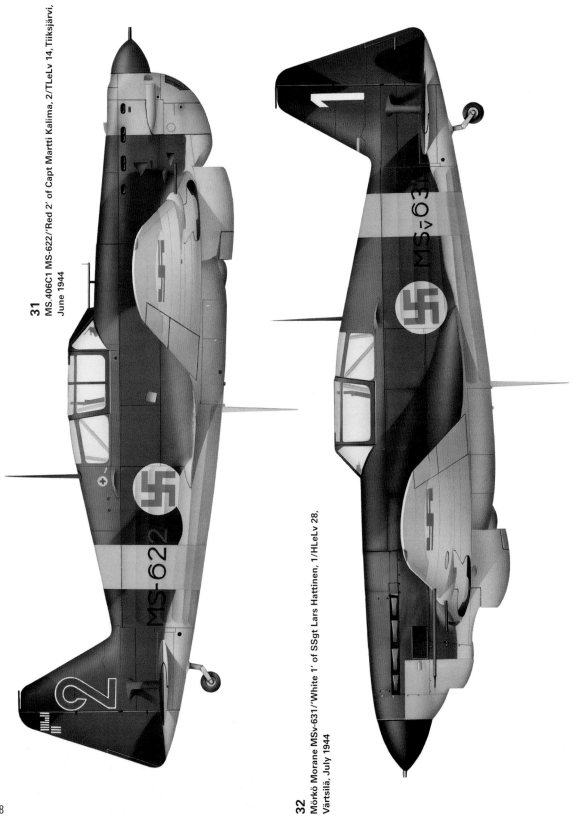

31
MS.406C1 MS-622/'Red 2' of Capt Martti Kalima, 2/TLeLv 14, Tiiksjärvi,
June 1944

32
Mörkö Morane MSv-631/'White 1' of SSgt Lars Hattinen, 1/HLeLv 28,
Värtsilä, July 1944

Cdt Maurice Arnoux (left) took part in many air races at the controls of various Caudron-Renault sport aeroplanes during the inter-war years. He also broke several world speed and altitude records (*via Author*)

This was the Order of Battle on 4 June at 1700 hrs;

Unit	Aircraft	Pilots	Location
GC III/1	29 (18)	14 pilots	Valence
GC I/2	unknown	unknown	Damblain
GC II/2	unknown	unknown	Chissey
GC I/6	22 (16)	16 pilots	Lognes-Émerainville
GC III/7	28 (19)	22 pilots	Orly

(The figures in brackets denote the number of immediately serviceable machines)

The *Armée de l'Air* claimed no fewer than 55 victories in 427 sorties on the first day of the Battle of France proper, but the archives show that only 23 German aircraft were lost. However, the French fighter pilots displayed both a heavy commitment and considerable aggression in a kind of swansong for the *Armée de l'Air*.

At 1800 hrs on 6 June a *patrouille* from GC III/7, led by Cdt Maurice Arnoux, left the Breguet 693s they were protecting to climb up and confront Bf 109s belonging to I./JG 1. After a ten-minute dogfight Maurice Arnoux dived to the ground, his aircraft's undercarriage down, obviously seeking a place to land. Probably wounded, he had partly lost control of his aircraft. The landing was hard and the aircraft bounced back into the air, flipped over on to its back and crash landed in a cornfield, near Angivillers. He was probably shot down by Hauptmann Wilhelm Balthasar. According to eyewitnesses, the Bf 109s strafed the wreck several times.

A few days later, German airmen came to his resting place to bury one of their own. Officers, after enquiring who this Frenchman was, paid him military honours and laid flowers on his grave. At 45, Arnoux was one of the oldest fighter pilots killed in World War 2.

On 8 June GC I/2 had a field day, claiming three Bf 109s and five Ju 87s for the loss of two Moranes and one pilot killed. According to

Cne Robert Williame chats with his wife (far right) and another patron of GC I/2 (a few years older than the Barbier sisters, though) at Beauvais-Tillé during the Phoney War (*via Author*)

German records only one Bf 109 (of 7./JG 3) and two Ju 87s (of I./St.G. 2) were lost to the French, which was still quite an achievement considering the Morane's poor capabilities. Cne Robert Williame was GC I/2's most successful pilot on this date, claiming three Bf 109s in just 15 seconds during his first sortie at around 1630 hrs;

'Over Beauvais I see three M 109s 400 m [440 yds] away from me heading northeast at 4500 m [1475 ft]) and six others that were part of a *patrouille triple*. I attack the first three, one after the other. Lt Chalupa, my wingman, fires just after me. The one on the right spins down in flames. Then I shoot at 30 m [33 yds] the one in the centre – sent it spinning down in flames. At the same distance I aim at the one on the left, which dives smoking. Duration of the combat – 15 seconds. Place – four to five kilometres [2.5-3 miles] northeast Beauvais.'

Taking off again at 1900 hrs, GC I/2 came upon a formation of Ju 87s from I./St.G. 2. Suddenly, as he was about to open fire, Williame had a great surprise;

'French roundels! I broke off without firing, but, having a doubt, I came back over them to ensure they did resemble the aeroplanes we had seen only in photographs. At the very moment I saw black crosses inside the roundels, the first Stuka pitched up and the rear gunner fired a short burst at me. I made a split-S and attacked it vertically from above. It dived at a steep angle, belching thick black smoke.'

Two Ju 87s were credited to Sgt Jacques de Puybusque as his sixth and seventh victories (both shared) – and his last ones. Aged 21, he was transferred to Indochina in February 1941 and killed in an accident in an MS.406 in June.

In his two sorties of the day, Williame claimed six successes (two shared). He wrote to his mother, 'As far as I am concerned, if my victories are confirmed, this will be a nice French record for me, for I have done it in 3 hrs 20 min exactly'.

The French pilots involved in this action on 8 June were adamant that the Stukas they engaged wore tricolour roundels. Given their overwhelming air superiority, it would have been most surprising for the Luftwaffe to have used such a trick, especially bearing in mind the Ju 87's unmistakable silhouette. There is little doubt that this was one of the first cases of numerous optical aberrations reported in almost all belligerent air forces during World War 2.

During the 8th numerous sorties were completed by *patrouilles simples* of GC II/2, GC I/6 and GC III/7 from Lognes-Émerainville, harassing armoured vehicles in the Forges-les-Eaux and Gournay areas from 0515 hrs until 1830 hrs. With its liquid-cooled engine, lack of armour and self-sealing tanks and light armament, the MS.406 was definitely not best suited to such a mission. Indeed, three Moranes of GC II/2 were shot down by flak and two pilots were killed (Cne Charles d'Abbadie d'Arrast and Adj Jacques Marconnet). GC I/6 lost one man and GC III/7 only one aircraft.

On 10 June, having brought down an Hs 126 near Connantre (shared between Gagnaire, Doublet and Sgt Roland Pélissier), a *patrouille double* of GC III/1 returned to their airfield at Rozay-en-Brie, flying low and slow to 'show the roundels' to French soldiers in accordance with orders. Unfortunately, the airfield had been overrun by German troops while the pilots had been aloft, and their deadly mobile flak batteries quickly shot

Gagnaire and Pélissier down in flames. The latter was wounded and taken prisoner, but Edgar Gagnaire was killed instantly.

Aged 33, Gagnaire had by then notched up seven kills, five of them shared. Oddly enough, at the medical examination when he first tried to enlist with the *Armée de l'Air* in 1929 he was declared 'definitely unfit as a fighter pilot'.

During the afternoon of 11 June GC III/1 was ordered to retreat to Valence, in southern France. All serviceable aircraft took off, but Doublet's engine refused to start. He was still standing by his Morane when German bombers arrived, dropping their ordnance on Rozay-en-Brie airfield. Kléber Doublet had his legs crushed by exploding bombs and died the next day in Sézanne hospital. For GC III/1 the war was almost over. A last kill was claimed on 19 June, before the unit was transferred to Orange-Caritat and, two days later, to Marseille-Marignane.

Although the personnel of GC I/2 were advised on 12 June that the unit was earmarked for conversion onto the new state-of-the-art French fighter, the Arsenal VG.33, their joy was short-lived. The *Groupe* began its long and painful retreat south the next day. It would soldier on to the bitter end with its outdated and worn-out Moranes.

At the ends of their tethers by 19 June, GC I/6 and GC III/7 pooled their aircraft under overall command of Cdt Louis Crémont of the latter unit at Bergerac. The end was near, and although GC III/7 was ordered to Toulouse on 22 June to collect D.520s, time had run out.

The *Aéronautique Navale* (French equivalent of the Royal Navy's Fleet Air Arm) activated *Escadrille* AC 5 at Hyères in mid June, and within a few days it had taken on 18 MS.406s handed over by the *Armée de l'Air*. All of them were worn out and many were unserviceable for lack of armament. However, at 1900 hrs on 20 June AC 5 carried out its first operational sortie, with six Moranes pursuing Do 17s that proved to be faster than the combat-weary French fighter, especially as they had already dropped their bombs.

Four days later, in one of its few missions with the MS.406, the *Aéronautique Navale* lost Second-Maître Henri Pivet of *Escadrille* AC 5, shot down by flak over Royan at about 1400 hrs.

Adj Jean Marchelidon poses with some pride by the wreckage of his only victory, which was also the ultimate success of the *Armée de l'Air* in the 1939-40 war. This Hs 126, belonging to 5.(H)/13, crashed at Beaumont-Monteux. Its pilot was killed and the observer mortally wounded. The total number of claims made by MS.406 units is still open to dispute – according to the official *Armée de l'Air* lists they accounted for 187 enemy aircraft (*via Author*)

Sometime after the armistice, a French airman (right) and an officer of the German Armistice Commission seem to bargain about the fate of MS.406 Nº786 abandonned 'somewhere in France'. It was eventually delivered to the Luftwaffe in 1942, but its subsequent fate is unknown. The Luftwaffe showed no interest in the Morane except as a 'low-cost' support to Finland (*via Author*)

That same day (24 June) strafing sorties were ordered to be undertaken by GC III/1, GC I/2, GC II/2 and GC I/6 in the Valence-Beaurepaire area, the high command hoping that the French fighters would slow the German advance down the Rhône Valley. Returning from his sortie, Adj Jean Marchelidon of GC I/2 caught sight of an Hs 126;

'Back to the east of Valence, at 6.10 pm, I spot on my right an aeroplane that flew up the Rhône River. I head towards it and I see it dive. I fly past it, it shoots at me and I notice black crosses. I recognise a Henschel 126. On my first pass, three-quarter astern, I see hits on its tailplane. I make three more passes – on the last one I shoot at point-blank range dead astern. I see the aeroplane enter a steep dive and hit the ground.'

The Hs 126, belonging to 5.(H)/13, crashed at Beaumont-Monteux. Its pilot had been killed and the observer mortally wounded. This Henschel proved to be the *Armée de l'Air's* last victory of the 1939-40 war.

However, over Valence-Beaurepaire, German flak had taken its toll. Miraculously, all of the aircraft of GC I/2 and GC II/2 returned home with varying degrees of battle damage, but GC III/1 and GC I/6 each lost a Morane. Sous-Lt Henri Raphenne of GC I/6 crashed near Romans and was found dead by German soldiers, who buried him with full military honours in a nearby cemetery. Raphenne, born in 1906, had claimed five confirmed victories (two shared). He was the last member of the *Armée de l'Air* to killed during the campaign. Symbolically, he was flying an MS.406.

On 25 June the armistice was enforced. France was divided into two parts – a so-called *Zone Libre* (free zone) mainly in southern France under the new Vichy government, which was subservient to Germany, and a *Zone Occupée* (occupied zone) mainly in northern France (including Paris), covering the whole of the French Atlantic and Channel and North Sea coasts.

According to the terms of the armistice the *Armée de l'Air* was to be disbanded, all of its aircraft being disabled as soon as possible to prevent them from being flown to England or Egypt.

UNDER VICHY AND THE RAF

How many MS.406s were lost in the 1939-40 campaign? This is a difficult question to answer, partly because the census demanded by the German and Italian Armistice Commissions was obviously false. Counting French aircraft after 25 June 1940 is an exercise in futility due to the inaccuracy of records following the armistice. However, 453 MS.406s were listed in the Free Zone, about 200 in northern Africa and about 50 in other territories (Syria-Lebanon and Indochina). So it appears that, from different causes (accidents, destruction by the enemy or abandonment), about 380 MS.406s were lost. This represents approximately 35 per cent of the production, a figure altogether comparable with the average the other French aircraft types (38 per cent).

Although the French Air Force was kept alive by the Germans thanks to its bold response to the shelling of the French fleet at Oran (Mers-el-Kébir) by the Royal Navy on 3-6 July, the MS.406 was phased out. The last units still equipped with this fighter were disbanded, their machines being stored, apart from GC I/7 in Syria-Lebanon and the two *escadrilles* based in French Indochina, both territories being loyal to Vichy. The latter were the first to bring their Morane's guns to bear.

INDOCHINA

Escadrille de Chasse 2/595 was formed at Bach Mai on 1 October 1939 with 12 of the 20 MS.406s disembarked at Saigon the previous month. Two problems soon arose. Firstly, there were few or no fighter pilots among the local airmen, which meant that the best aviators in-theatre had to undergo a specific training course prior to them being given the MS.406 to fly. Secondly, there were no spare parts in Indochina, and cannibalisation could only be performed after the first accidents had occurred.

On 22 September 1940 a border incident was caused by Japanese troops patrolling around the French outpost at Lang-Son. A small war raged for four days, with Moranes playing a minor role by escorting Potez 25TOE reconnaissance biplanes. It was hoped that their presence would act as a deterrent for Japanese Nakajima Ki-27 'Nate' fighters. On the last day of hostilities Sgt Williame Labussière, flying as wingman for Adj-chef Tivollier, spotted a hostile twin-engined aeroplane over Ha-Gi. Labussière relates;

In the Free Zone no operational unit was equipped with the Morane between June 1940 and December 1942. However, a score of machines were kept airworthy for training. These MS.406s have just been withdrawn from storage at Châteauroux and are ready to be flown to Salon-de-Provence, where they will be used by the prestigious *École de l'Air* – a school training fighter instructors under the command of Cne Jean-Mary Accart, a Curtiss ace who had claimed 12 victories with GC I/5 in 1940. The aircraft wearing the tactical code *XXXIV* is N°945, inherited from GC I/2. All aeroplanes wear the standard 'Vichy' markings consisting of garish yellow and red stripes (*ECPA-D*)

Sgt Williame Labussière added to his earlier claims in Spain and China by downing a Japanese twin-engined bomber over Indochina. However, this victory was officially denied by the French authorities, who were afraid of causing another incident with the Japanese (*via Author*)

'I waved at Tivollier, who did not understand my signal but showed me by sign language that we had to turn back. I did not agree. Diving on the aeroplane, I identified it at once as Japanese. It had no reason to be there. I gave a warning shot ahead of it. Immediately, the rear gunner opened fire and I was surrounded by bullets. This time I pressed the trigger for good and set its left engine ablaze. The pilot manoeuvred with great skill to reach a cloud and it was gone from my sight. With too little fuel for a chase, I made it for home.

'Cne Gangloff [commander of EC 2/595] was delighted to hear this good news. We were ordered not to open fire except for self-defence. Obviously, I had acted in self-defence, he added, smiling. However, I had no idea of the fate of my alleged victim. It would not be long before I knew. A couple of days later an army truck arrived at Bach Mai and unloaded a motley collection of metal parts and armament. I asked the sergeant who was in charge where all this stuff came from. He answered that it was secret, and that he was not allowed to speak. However, through an indiscretion I learned the debris was parts of a Japanese bomber – "my" bomber!

'I required authorisation to record this victory in my log book, and my capitaine wrote a report for the attention of the staff. That was when the shit hit the fan! A few days later a staff officer came to Bach Mai and summoned the two of us. We got bawled out in the harshest way and my log book was confiscated. When I got it back, the entry regarding my mission had been scratched out in red ink, although my victory was still clearly legible. However, officially, nothing had happened!'

Such was the obedience of the Vichy authorities to the Axis powers.

Born in 1912, William Labussière did his military service as a would-be fighter pilot. He was living on the Ivory Coast when he decided to take part in the Spanish Civil War, but not with the International Brigades or with Malraux, but as a regular pilot of the Republican Air Force. Singled out by the Soviets, who praised him as a 'true fighter pilot', he was given the opportunity to lead a squadron of Polikarpov I-16s to protect Carthagena and the surrounding airfields. However, in August 1937, fed up with the Soviet propaganda that surrounded its support of the Republican cause, Labussière left the force.

The following month he enlisted in Claire Chennault's American Volunteer Group in China, where he flew Dewoitine D.510s with the 41st Pursuit Squadron and even Vultee V-11 bombers. When war broke out in Europe Labussière cancelled his contract and moved to Indochina, where he enlisted in the *Armée de l'Air* as a sergent. Caught trying to join the US forces in August 1941, he was sentenced to five years of forced labour for high treason. Up to late 1944, when he eventually fled to China, his life in Vichy French jails was an indescribable hell.

After the ceasefire the French conceded the transfer of Hanoi Harbour and a few airfields, which the Japanese would put to good use a year or so later to sink the British capital ships HMS *Prince of Wales* and HMS *Repulse*. Thailand (or Siam, as the country was still called at that time) had now regained enough confidence to demand the return of territories annexed by the French at the turn of the century. Soon the Thais and the French began violating each other's airspace and, one thing leading to another, war would soon break out.

On 10 October 1940 *Escadrille de Chasse* 2/596 was formed and equipped with MS.406s that had either been withdrawn from storage or transferred from EC 2/595. When conflict with Siam flared up, EC 2/595 was sent to Dong Hene (in Laos) and EC 2/596 to Siem Reap, adjoining the famous Angkor Wat temple in Cambodia.

On 1 December *Aéronautique Navale* pilots Premier Maître (Chief Petty Officer) André Châtel and Maître (Petty Officer) Jean Mouligné of EC 2/596 clashed with three Thai Vought Curtiss Hawk IIIs near Nakhon Phanom and damaged one of them. Châtel was credited with an enemy aeroplane 'out of commission'. On 9 December an encounter occurred between three MS.406s and Thai V-93S Corsairs. The Thais claimed a French aeroplane destroyed, but Châtel did not share their point of view;

'We were bounced by three Corsairs coming from higher up. However, they had not gone unnoticed and we eluded their first pass. I engaged in a dogfight with one, which tried to drive me to a lower altitude where it could put its better manoeuvrability to good use. While continuing to battle with my opponents, I started to climb and the Siamese carelessly followed me. We went up to 4000 m [13,100 ft], where the power of my Hispano-Suiza made up for my handicap in terms of manoeuvrability. After two or three turns one of them was in front of my gunsight, and I opened fire from three-quarters astern. It was hit and bullets set fire to its tank. It went down in a slow spin, engulfed in flames and smoke. I did not bother about its fate, as my wingmen needed a hand.'

The Thais acknowledged the destruction of the Corsair, shot down in flames near Lakhon.

Meanwhile, Mouligné was struggling with the other two Corsairs. Châtel came to his rescue, and the two Frenchmen damaged one of the remaining enemy fighters before the Thais broke away and crossed back over the Mekong. The Moranes were then attacked by a lone Curtiss Hawk III of No 70 Sqn, the Frenchmen turning the tables and wounding the pilot prior to him fleeing for home.

On 4 January 1941 EC 2/595 was relieved by EC 2/596 at Dong Hene. That evening, a raid by six Corsairs destroyed one Morane and severely damaged another. On 8 January the French met a new adversary, the Mitsubishi Ki-30 'Ann', dubbed 'Nagoya' by the Thais, 24 of which had been handed over by the Japanese to the Royal

Premier Maître André Châtel (right) and Maître Jean Mouligné (left) in a theatrical pose for the camera at Dong Hene in November 1940. MS.406 N°306 of EC 2/596 has yet to have its unit badge applied within the shield on the fighter's fin. Châtel and Labussière of the *Aéronautique Navale* were the only 'true' fighter pilots in French Indochina at that time (*via Author*)

Thai Air Force a few days before the outbreak of war with France. On 10 January four Moranes led by Adj-chef Tivollier intercepted nine 'Nagoyas' and two Curtiss H-75Ns that were bombing Siem Reap. Tivollier claimed both fighters. In fact, they did manage to return home, but one Ki-30 *was* shot down.

A ceasefire was ordered by Japan on 28 January at 1000 hrs. Needless to say, under pressure from Japan, the French had to yield large parts of Indochina to Thailand. The Moranes had flown 52 sorties (203 hrs) and officially lost two of their number. In fact, only 14 remained airworthy.

In February 1941 a few 'true' fighter pilots arrived from France, including Lt Maurice Hutter (who had claimed one victory in an MB.152 with GC II/1 prior to being wounded in the left arm by return fire from a Do 17 on 19 May 1940), Sgt-chef Jacques de Puybusque, who has been mentioned earlier, and Cne Pierre Pouyade, who previously flew Potez 631 nightfighters. They were the last reinforcements sent from France. Indochina had not received any new aircraft or spare parts since late 1939, and it would never do so. In July 1941 EC 2/596 was disbanded and Cne Pierre Pouyade took over command of EC 2/595.

On 27 January 1942 an American raid took place on Hanoi. Three Moranes were scrambled, but they deliberately took a reciprocal course so as not to tangle with what the pilots considered friendly forces. However, in doing so they flew too close to Japanese airspace and three Ki-27s of the 84th Dokuritsu Hikô Chutai were directed to intercept them. Because of the so-called 'Vichy markings' on the Moranes, comprising yellow and red stripes, they were allegedly mistaken for American fighters, Lt Maurice Hutter recalled;

'We saw them dive upon us and, knowing their habit of shooting on sight at anything that flew, I made a sign to my wingmen to break off and run away. Unfortunately the Japanese had the double benefit of height and speed, and they easily caught up with our puffing Moranes. Delisle, hoping they would recognise their mistake, waggled his wings and even lowered his undercarriage. His aircraft caught fire at the first burst. He just had time to bail out. Bassaget and I had no other choice than to face them.

'The combat was already lost. Their nimble monoplanes were much faster than ours on their last legs. My weapons jammed at the first burst. I saw Bassaget fall in flames. Not wishing to share his fate, I dived to the ground and pulled out at the last moment. Two Japanese had followed me. I hit a tree with my left wingtip. The aeroplane crabbed along and came down in a field of sugar cane. Contact was rough and I was ejected out of the cockpit. In a semi-unconscious state, I crawled away and ducked into a rice field. The Japanese made three or four passes to strafe the burning wreck.'

Adj-chef Bassaget was killed and Sgt-chef Delisle injured, while Hutter suffered contusions. The Japanese CO, Maj Nagumo Tsunao, drove to Tong to apologise and even visited the two pilots in hospital.

That was the last action seen by MS.406s in Indochina. The last remaining machines were soon put of commission one after another owing to a lack of spares, with cannibalisation eventually showing its limits. However, the 'desertion' of Pouyade sealed the fate of the last Moranes, which were grounded by order of the Japanese authorities.

SYRIA

As recounted previously in this chapter, GC I/7 had been transferred to Lebanon in March 1940 and was kept in the Vichy French Order of Battle by the German Armistice Commission. In early May 1941 the Germans, who wanted to help insurgents force the British out of Iraq, received Vichy approval to land and refuel transport aeroplanes in Syria. However, the British were not in a *laissez-faire* mood. On 14 May Bristol Blenheims and Curtiss Tomahawks strafed German aircraft at Palmyra. It was the start of a new conflict between the RAF and the *Armée de l'Air de l'Armistice*.

In the early phase of the conflict the latter had only 20 Moranes to defend a 1000 km-long (620-mile) border between Syria and the British territories of Palestine, Transjordan and Iraq. On 18 May they attempted to intercept incoming bombers. Ten days later, Sous-Lt André Vuillemin shot down a Blenheim near Aleppo.

On 8 June Commonwealth and Free French troops crossed the border in Operation *Exporter*. Two *Groupes* equipped with D.520s, hurriedly sent to Lebanon and Syria, were to bear the brunt of the air defence. However, GC I/7 kept on fighting. Two 'Blenheims' were claimed by Adj-chef Georges Amarger on 4 and 7 July, the second, which was actually a Vickers Wellington of No 80 Sqn, being noteworthy as the only night victory credited to a French fighter pilot during World War 2. Amarger added a third victory to his tally while flying a Spitfire in April 1945.

This campaign, as any other fought by the French between 1940 and 1942, ended in an armistice on 14 July 1941.

MADAGASCAR

Madagascar had remained loyal to the Vichy Government. This isolated island in the Indian Ocean, thousands of miles away from France and facing the British territories of southeast Africa, had little or no military aviation, apart from a handful of peacekeeping squadrons flying antiquated biplanes. Several military airfields had been built long before World War 2, the key one being Diego Arrachart, close to Diego Suarez — one of the largest natural harbours in the world that was comparable with Pearl Harbor or Scapa Flow.

On 7 January 1941 *Escadrille* 565 was formed in anticipation of 17 MS.406s being shipped from France. The first three machines were disembarked in October. In January 1942 *Escadrille* 565 moved with its 17 Moranes to Ivato, near the capital, Tananarive. A month later this *escadrille* merged with another equipped with Potez 63.11s to become the *Groupe Aérien Mixte* (GAM).

Fearing that Madagascar might supply Japanese submarines on their journeys to the French Atlantic coast (which indeed happened), the

One more snapshot for home. Australian soldiers smile for the camera behind the tail of MS.406 Nº762, lined up with the last survivors of GC I/7 at Aleppo-Nerab in July 1941. This particular aircraft was flown by Cne Georges Escudier, the unit's deputy CO, who was authorised to have the badges of both *escadrilles* applied to the fin of his fighter (*Australian War Memorial*)

57

Lt Michel Laurant's MS.406, N°842, after his forced landing following an encounter with Fleet Air Arm Martlets on 7 May 1942. A South African soldier added this snapshot to his photo album before going back home (*SAAF via Mike Schoeman*)

British High Command decided to respond to the threat by instigating Operation *Ironclad*, but it confined the campaign's objective to the capture of Diego Suarez. Apart from three South African Air Force (SAAF) Flights forming No 20 SAAF Sqn (22 Martin Marylands and Bristol Beauforts), the British counted upon two aircraft carriers, HMS *Illustrious* and HMS *Indomitable*, and the 20 Grumman Martlet IIs of 881 and 882 Naval Air Squadrons (NASs) aboard the former.

In the meantime the GAM had despatched 13 MS.406s to Diego Arrachart, and these were to bear the brunt of the British onslaught, which started on 5 May 1942. Albacores from *Indomitable* destroyed five Moranes on the ground, the remainder being withdrawn to Anivorano and Ambilobé. At 1630 hrs three MS.406s took off to strafe the landing beaches, and one of them mysteriously disappeared – no claim was submitted by any Royal Navy unit.

At dawn on 7 May Martlets of 881 NAS and four Moranes were patrolling the same area south of Diego Suarez. They inevitably met. The British counted two pairs of Moranes, and Lt Cdr John C Cockburn made a head-on pass on the first pair. He took a few 20 mm rounds in his aircraft's engine and wings. Probably hit by Cne Leonetti, Cockburn crash landed in Courrier Bay. Sub-Lt J A Lyon followed his leader into the attack, but changed his mind on seeing the 'first pair' on his heels. He shot one down before the top cover entered the fray and brought down two more Moranes.

Three MS.406s were indeed lost to the Martlets, Leonetti managing to bail out, Lt Michel Laurant force landing and Cne Jean Bernache-Assollant being killed. Better known in France as Assollant for short, Bernache-Assollant was very famous during the interwar years, particularly for his transatlantic flight between Paris and New York in 1929. Aged 35, he had also claimed two kills flying D.520s with GC III/6 in June 1940.

This was the sole air-to-air combat of the whole campaign. The French surrendered at Diego Suarez late on the morning of 7 May. Hostilities

were resumed on 10 September 1942. As far as is known, at that time only two MS.406s were still airworthy. Operating from various secondary airfields in the savannah, they played hide-and-seek with the SAAF until only one, number 815, was left owing to a lack of spares. The ultimate recorded operational flight of the last Morane was a reconnaissance over Betroka on 20 October, flown by Sgt André Largeau, a pilot who had claimed one victory in an MB.152 in May 1940 and who would add two more with *Escadrille Normandie* before being killed on 14 September 1943. Madagascar was entirely conquered on 6 November 1942.

MS.406 N°819 was flown by Cne Jean Tulasne, who escaped from Lebanon in December 1940. It still wears the insignia of GC I/7 on the fuselage, but all French national markings have been overpainted with British roundels. The fighter is shown here at Haifa whilst serving with No 2 French Fighter Flight. Note the Potez 63.11 in the background (*via Author*)

ON THE BRITISH SIDE

In late June 1940, the British required help from the French to reinforce their defences in Egypt. On 23 June GC I/7 sent three MS.406s to El Amira via Ismailia. Two days later France signed an armistice with Germany and the three pilots were summoned to return to Lebanon. However, they chose to stay and fight on with the RAF. On 8 July the two remaining Moranes formed the No 2 French Fighter Flight (FFF), together with two Potez 63.11s that had also 'deserted'. The Moranes received British insignia and serials (AX674 and AX675). It must be noted that the pilots (and mechanics) never enlisted in the Free French Air Force and were incorporated into the RAF like many other foreign personnel.

Initially, No 2 FFF became C Flight of No 80 Sqn and then of No 274 Sqn in Alexandria in late August. It was then sent to Haifa, where the flight was joined by Cne Jean Tulasne of GC I/7, who had fled from Lebanon with his MS.406 on 5 December. Tulasne was to be the first CO of *Escadrille Normandie* on the Russian Front. He was killed in action on 17 July 1943. In late December all FFF personnel were sent back to Egypt to train on Hurricanes.

The last airworthy MS.406s served as trainers in Syria between September 1941 and May 1942, when the French pilots were divided into two contingents – *Groupe de Chasse* No 1 *Alsace*, to be engaged in Libya, and *Escadrille de Chasse* No 3 *Normandie*, bound for the Soviet Union.

THE WINTER WAR

On the last day of November 1939 the Soviet Union launched its land, sea and air offensive against Finland. The main front was at the Karelian Isthmus, where the Soviet 7th Army force of more than ten divisions attacked five Finnish divisions. Between Lake Ladoga and Porajärvi the 8th Army was opposed by two divisions of Finnish troops. Further north, in the directions of Kantalahti and Uhtua, the 9th Army attacked, while the 14th Army advanced from Murmansk. In these regions the Finns could muster only detached battalions – three opposing the 9th Army and another three the 14th Army. The Red Banner Baltic Fleet, the Lake Ladoga Naval Detachment and the Arctic Fleet protected the flanks of the Soviet armies.

At the beginning of this conflict, which became known worldwide as the Winter War, the Soviets had 2318 aircraft concentrated on the Finnish front, while the *Ilmavoimat* could muster only 114 aircraft, of which 45 were fighters. Of these, just 35 were reasonably modern Fokker D.XXIs (see *Osprey Aircraft of the Aces 112 – Fokker D.XXI Aces of World War 2* for further details).

The war ended in the peace treaty of Moscow on 13 March 1940. Although Finland had lost huge areas of land by then, it remained unconquered and independent. By the end the conflict the Soviets possessed 3818 aircraft and the Finns 166, 100 of these being fighters.

Immediately after fighting had broken out on 30 November 1939, the Finnish purchasing commissions frantically went in search of combat aircraft, like many other nations at that time. Military materiel became harder to obtain, and prices escalated. Finland's position was becoming more and more alarming under the threat of the Soviet Union, and instructions were issued to buy any fighter aircraft that could be found. Authorised by the Finnish government, ambassadors in Britain and France approached those countries' respective governments for any kind of war materiel, especially aircraft that could quickly be made operational.

In Britain the Air Ministry had already agreed on 5 December 1939 to supply second-line aircraft to Finland, and a week later the first contract was signed between the Gloster Aircraft Company and the Finnish government. In this way the British government avoided a potential political confrontation with the Soviet Union. Finland did not care how the deals were made. Much more important was the availability of aircraft and other equipment. Similar contracts with other aircraft manufacturers were soon to follow.

France was not so particular about its political image, and the French military attaché in Helsinki received a telegram on 28 December 1939 informing him that the French government had initially decided to donate 50 fighters to Finland, in addition to airfield equipment, spares, coolants and 1.35 million rounds of ammunition. The list was later expanded following the addition of 80 Caudron-Renault CR.714 and 46 Koolhoven FK.58 fighters and 62 Potez 633 bombers.

Shortly after the Winter War had ended Prime Minister Edouard Daladier informed the French Parliament that the nation had donated 145 aircraft and plenty of other war materiel to Finland. In fact only 36 aircraft ever arrived.

Of the 50 promised MS.406 fighters, only 30 were drawn from Air Depot 304, packed in crates and shipped from 10 January 1940 onwards to Malmö, Sweden, for assembly. On 17 January Cne Raoul Etienne's group of seven Frenchmen (six technicians and a test pilot) arrived at the Aerotransport facilities at Malmö. At the same time the crated aircraft began reaching Sweden. On 19 January assembly commenced, and the first Morane was ready for delivery ten days later.

In addition to covered national insignia, the *Ilmavoimat* serials MS301 to MS330 inclusive (now without the dash) were applied, both on the rear fuselage and under the wings, and sometimes also on the wing uppersurfaces. The Moranes were then flown to Västerås, in central Sweden, for collection by Finnish pilots. The first two departed for Finland on 4 February 1940, and all 30 were picked up in lots of two to five aircraft by the end of the month.

New Squadron

Lentolaivue (LLv) 28 was established on 8 December 1939, with Maj Niilo Jusu in command. The flight leaders were Capt Sven-Erik Sirén (1st), 1Lt Reino Turkki (2nd) and Capt Eino Jutila (3rd). Based at Säkylä in southwestern Finland, the squadron was tasked with the protection of vital ports in this area. The unit began building up in strength prior to the arrival of new fighters in Finland, which three weeks later were known to be MS.406s donated by France.

On 2 February the first two Moranes arrived at the squadron's base, and by the end of the month all 30 had been received. At this point the MS.406s were armed with only three 7.5 mm machine guns, as the engine-mounted 20 mm cannon did not reach LLv 28 for a further three months.

Wasting no time, the unit performed its first combat mission from Säkylä on 6 February 1940, flying in the defence of Turku and other southwestern ports. Eleven days later the Morane pilots drew first blood, sending a bomber down over the southwestern archipelago. Future ace 1Lt Tuomo Hyrkki and his wingman had intercepted nine Ilyushin DB-3 bombers over Pori, and Hyrkki, flying MS301, repeatedly attacked the leftmost aeroplane. He finally caused it to emit smoke, and it went down on the ice south of the Utö Lighthouse. He also silenced the dorsal gunners of two other bombers. Hyrkki's victim had belonged to 53rd DBAP (Long-Range Bomber Aviation Regiment), which confirmed the loss.

At 1100 hrs, on 20 February, the Moranes shot down two of six Tupolev SB bombers approaching the port of Rauma. 1Lts Reino Turkki and Mikko Linkola claimed the left wingmen of both three-aircraft formations, the bombers crashing in flames on the ice outside Rauma. Three hours later, future ace 1Lt Veikko Karu, flying MS321, chased nine DB-3s of 53rd DBAP towards Estonia. He caught up with the formation just as they reached the Estonian coast, sending two of them down. This engagement had been a real test of Karu's physical endurance since the chase had taken place at an altitude of 7000 m (23,000 ft), and the Finn had no oxygen mask, thus making it very difficult for him to breathe in

MS.406 MS318 of 2/LLv 28 at Säkylä, in southwestern Finland, in early March 1940. Its tactical number on the fin is a yellow 3. The silver-coloured star on the rudder denoted future ace 2Lt Pauli Massinen's victory over a DB-3 bomber on 2 March. In front of the aeroplane are French mechanics Decousser and Levard (*Pauli Massinen*)

the rarefied air. Such tenacity would win Karu the Mannerheim Cross (Finland's highest award for bravery in action) 18 months later.

By March, when the Soviet advance had seemed to halt at the Finnish Army's rearmost defensive line on the Karelian Isthmus, southeast of Viipuri (Vyborg), the Red Armies decided to attack the rear of the defences by crossing the frozen Gulf of Vyborg. Along other sections of the frontline the Soviet advance had ended earlier, and north of Lake Ladoga communist troops, facing slow starvation, fiercely defended their encircled positions. The Soviets tried to advance to the rear of the Finns to help break the encirclements, but these efforts failed.

On 2 March LLv 28 claimed three bombers in southwestern Finland, and in a chase towards Estonia a Polikarpov I-153 fighter was also caught and shot down. Future aces 2Lt Pauli Massinen in MS318 and Cpl Urho Lehtovaara in MS326 both claimed their first kills on this date.

The Soviets had observed the presence of new fighters in southwestern Finland, with units of the Baltic Fleet air forces claiming to have destroyed six Brewster Buffaloes in the Turku area on 2 March. Both the type and numbers were pure fiction, as the Finns did not lose a single aeroplane on that date, and the Brewsters had not yet arrived in-theatre in any case. The new aeroplanes encountered by the Soviet aviators were Moranes, which two days later were misidentified as Spitfires. But knowledge of the Brewsters' imminent delivery to the *Ilmavoimat* meant that the Soviets had spies in Sweden monitoring what was going on in assembly plants or at transit airfields in the neutral country.

On 4 March Soviet troops managed to cross the Gulf of Vyborg and form a bridgehead near Finnish territory. Troops and columns flowed across the ice, and all *Ilmavoimat* units were thrown into action against this serious threat. By 7 March the situation had become critical, and two flights of Moranes from LLv 28 were transferred to Hollola, closer to the front on the Karelian Isthmus. They immediately joined in the strafing attacks over the Gulf of Vyborg. Three days later the advance on the ice had been blunted owing to heavy losses caused by the combined efforts of Finnish strafing missions and coastal artillery.

The last combats were fought over southern Finland on 11 March, when Soviet fighter formations numbering as many as 200 aircraft were observed. For its last victories of the Winter War LLv 28 claimed three DB-3s from 7th DBAP, with future aces 2Lts Martti Inehmo and Aarre Linnamaa opening their scores.

At 1100 hrs on 13 March the Winter War ended with the peace negotiated in Moscow. LLv 28 had flown 288 sorties with its MS.406s, claiming 14 aerial victories and losing one aircraft, but no pilots.

The Soviet units had flown 100,970 sorties, claiming 427 aerial victories for the loss of 261 aircraft according to official records from 1939-40. The losses have since been adjusted by modern research to 388 aircraft – 188 fighters, 146 bombers and 54 aircraft of the Baltic Fleet air forces. By comparison, the *Ilmavoimat* had flown 5693 sorties, claimed 207 aircraft destroyed and lost 53 warplanes on operations. Finnish anti-aircraft guns had been credited with a further 314 Soviet aircraft.

MORE MORANES

After the German occupation of France in late June 1940, the Finns commenced negotiations with the German authorities to buy war-booty materiel, including captured aircraft. On 1 October 1940 a contract was duly signed between the Finnish and German governments. It included sale of war-booty to Finland in return for the transit of German troops and supplies via Finland to northern Norway, which the Wehrmacht had occupied in the spring of 1940.

Under this agreement ten captured MS.406s were bought. Having arrived in crates by 4 January 1941, they were assembled and overhauled by the State Aircraft Factory and received the codes MS-601 to MS-610.

On 13 March 1940 – the last day of the Winter War – MS305 of 3/LLv 28 takes off from Pyhäniemi ice airstrip at Hollola. The latter was used as a base from which strafing missions against Russian troops crossing the frozen Viipurinlahti (Gulf of Vyborg) could be generated. 3/LLv 28 applied white tactical numbers to the fins of its MS.406s (*SA-kuva*)

MS329 of LLv 28 at Naarajärvi in the spring of 1941. The tactical numbers worn by the unit's MS.406s were changed with the Continuation War mobilisation of 17 June 1941, this particular fighter being marked with a yellow 1. It was in this guise that the aircraft was flown by future 6.5-victory ace Cpl Toivo Tomminen of 3/LLv 28 in the latter half of 1941. Indeed, he claimed the last of his kills (a Hurricane) in MS329 on 4 December 1941 (*Finnish War Museum*)

By the end of 1941 another 15 aircraft had been obtained. The first three arrived in June, seven more were received in August and the remainder in November, their serials being MS-611 to MS-625 inclusive.

BOMBER OFFENSIVE

Operation *Barbarossa*, the German invasion of the Soviet Union (decided upon in December 1940), was planned to begin after the spring thaw. A delay was caused by the occupation of Yugoslavia and the Balkans, so the start of *Barbarossa* was postponed to 22 June 1941. By this time the Germans had by various means persuaded Hungary, Rumania and Finland to side with them, as they had borders with the Soviet Union or close to it. The operation was revealed to Finnish military leaders only four weeks before its launch. Following receipt of this information, Finnish forces were mobilised on 17 June 1941.

Just before the offensive commenced large numbers of German aircraft were based on airfields in southern Finland, carrying out missions such as reconnaissance and channel mining. Soviet Intelligence quickly discovered their presence on Finnish airfields, and the Russians assumed that these bases would also be used for major attacks on Leningrad. They therefore decided to attack these airfields first, and drew up a plan for a six-day offensive bombardment.

The key assets involved in these raids would be aircraft from the Leningrad Military District, parts of the Baltic Military District and the Northern and Baltic Fleets, which, combined, had 2503 warplanes at their disposal from the Arctic Sea to the Baltic Sea. Some 933 of these aircraft were bombers and 1327 were fighters. In addition, a further 202 long-range bombers were held in the rear. The operational border between Germany and Finland ran along the Oulu-Kajaani-Belomorsk line, and south of it half of the communist force could be directed against Finland.

The first Morane victory (an SB bomber) of the Continuation War was claimed by Sgt Antti Tani of 1/LLv 28 on 25 June 1941, flying his assigned aircraft, MS311. The fighter is seen here at Lunkula in September 1941 with its mechanics, R Tuomela and U Alanen. The last victory marked on the MS.406's fin is dated 23 August 1941 (*Author's collection*)

Soviet air raids began early in the morning of 25 June 1941. During the course of the day the Russians flew 263 bomber and 224 fighter sorties, attacking several locations in southern and southwestern Finland, including airfields and purely civilian targets. After these bombardments the parliament considered Finland to be in a state of war with the communists and declared war on the Soviet Union. Thus the Continuation War began.

LLv 28, assigned to *Lentorykmentti* (LeR) 2, was then based at Naarajärvi and commanded by Capt Sven-Erik Sirén. It had 27 serviceable Moranes in three flights, led by Capt Timo Tanskanen (1st) and 1Lts Reino Turkki (2nd) and Erkki Lupari (3rd). The unit's task at this point was to protect the mobilisation of the field army in southeastern Finland.

On 25 June large bomber formations were first seen entering the airspace of southern Finland from observation posts in Turku at 0600 hrs. The Soviet targets in southeastern Finland were the airfields at Joensuu and Joroinen. Although LLv 28 was based away from these sites, the 1st Flight patrol met a lone, apparently disoriented, SB bomber of 10th SBAP (Fast Bomber Aviation Regiment) and shot it down at 1300 hrs. Future ace Sgt Antti Tani described his first kill thus;

'I observed the enemy aeroplane at 1800 m [5900 ft] altitude over Rantasalmi, about 15 km [nine miles] west of the railway, flying in the direction of 135 degrees. Right after seeing the aircraft I banked after it. When I got to within 50-75 metres [55-80 yds] of it I opened fire from right behind, aiming on a line from the dorsal gunner to the port engine. Immediately after firing the engine burst into flames, but not for long, leaving only a thick smoke trail from the engine. I fired another three bursts without additional effect. Cpl Pauli Lehtonen saw the aeroplane come down. My aeroplane was MS311.'

Moranes of 3/LLv 28 at Naarajärvi, in southeastern Finland, on 28 June 1941. Aircraft MS-603 was flown by future five-kill ace 1Lt Jouko Myllymäki, who would claim his second victory (an SB bomber) in it on 26 September 1941. Behind the Morane are MS318 and MS-325. The latter was the mount of future 6.5-victory ace Sgt Toivo Tomminen. The tail numbers on these machines were applied in yellow, often with a thin red outline (*SA-kuva*)

The *Ilmavoimat* fighters downed 26 Soviet bombers on the first day (23 later admitted by the Soviets), which was a promising start for the Continuation War. However, these attacks had highlighted major gaps in the Finnish air-surveillance and fighter-control systems. Although 121 fighters were ready to intercept, only one fifth of them could be directed to deal with the enemy. The weak spots in the system were quickly detected and put into sound working order.

The Soviet bombing offensive against Finland lasted six days (from 25 to 30 June), during which time Finnish and German air bases were attacked on 39 occasions with a total of 992 aircraft. Bomber crews claimed the destruction of 130 Axis aircraft on the ground and in the air. The Luftwaffe suffered no losses, however, as its aircraft had already left these airfields. Finnish losses were two slightly damaged aircraft. On the other hand, fighter pilots from the *Ilmavoimat* claimed to have shot down 34 Russian bombers during the same period.

After this offensive the Soviets transferred most of the units stationed on the Finnish front south to repel the rapid German advance. On the Finnish sector, after the regrouping, the communists had the 23rd Army on the Karelian Isthmus and the 7th Army north of Lake Ladoga, with responsibility for the front up to Uhtua in the direction of the White Sea. The air forces of the 23rd Army consisted of 5th SAD (Combined Aviation Division) with two fighter and two assault regiments –7th and 153rd IAPs (Fighter Aviation Regiments) and 65th and 235th ShAPs (Ground-attack Aviation Regiments). In August 1941 65th ShAP was transferred to the 7th Army air forces. The latter controlled 55th SAD with one bomber and four fighter regiments (72nd SBAP and 155th, 179th, 197th and 415th IAPs, plus 65th ShAP from August 1941 onwards).

On 3 July the pilot of a Morane from 2/LLv 28 fired all of his ammunition into one DB-3 bomber, sending it down. Sgt Urho Lehtovaara submitted two combat reports following this encounter. Here is the latter one, after the wreck of the aircraft had been found three weeks later;

2/LLv 28's MS-602 undergoes gun harmonisation at Joensuu in July 1941. This was the first assigned aeroplane of future eight-victory MS.406 ace 2Lt Martti Inehmo. On 9 July its fin was adorned with a victory bar denoting Inehmo's first Continuation War kill, over a MiG-3. On 8 August MS-602 was damaged when it hit a camouflaged barn at Joensuu (*Pauli Massinen*)

'Flying at 3000 metres [9800 ft], I observed at 1135 hrs three aircraft bombing Joensuu airfield. I signalled the lead aeroplane (1Lt Massinen) and instantly commenced the chase. After seven minutes I caught up with the enemy bombers and began firing at the aircraft on the right wing [of the formation]. The gunner of the middle aeroplane fired at me all the time, and for safety reasons I put a burst into him, silencing the position.

'I continued to fire at the original target, putting all my ammunition into it, then the starboard undercarriage fell down. Mechanic Nisula confirmed the similarity of the damage in the wreck, which was found east of Ilomantsi. My aeroplane was MS327.'

On 9 July 1Lt Pauli Massinen's swarm of 2/LLv 28 fighters was engaged in a combat at Räisälä with five MiG-3 fighters, shooting two down. On the return flight five SB bombers were observed and two were destroyed, in spite of interference by the escort fighters. Sgt Lehtovaara claimed a triple between 1440 hrs and 1500 hrs;

'After observing five enemy fighters I signalled my lead aircraft and dived instantly towards the enemy fighter. I entered immediately into a turning battle and after five minutes got a burst to hit the enemy fighter, which instantly dived to the ground, catching fire. After breaking off I flew towards Elisenvaara, one enemy fighter following me. After arriving at Lumivaara I observed five enemy SB bombers, which flew in a tight echelon straight to the west. I attacked the wing aircraft on the right flank and shot at its starboard engine, which immediately caught fire, and the bomber crashed into the ground.

'The enemy fighter that was following me fired at me all the time and pulled over me, banking to the right. After noticing that I was being left alone for a while, I moved again behind the wingman of the right flank of the bomber formation and fired a short burst into its fuselage and next to the starboard engine, which caught fire. The aeroplane dived in flames into the forest.

'The remaining three bombers then changed to a northeasterly course.

'The enemy fighter followed me up to Elisenvaara, where it turned to the south. I could not participate in combat since I had run out of machine gun ammunition. The I-17 (MiG-3) was faster than my aeroplane, but less manoeuvrable, being armed with heavy machine guns or cannons.

'My aeroplane was MS327.'

FINNISH ADVANCE

On 10 July the Karelian Army offensive commenced from the Kitee-Ilomatsi area towards the northwestern coast of Lake Ladoga. The CO of LeR 2 specified that the operational areas for LLv 24 and LLv 28 were Saarivaara-Korpijärvi-Kolosenjärvi-Mannervaara-Tohmajärvi-Pälkjärvi-Kakunvaara-Kaurila-Matkaselkä. The two units were to take it in turns to maintain air superiority in these areas.

On 16 July the VI Army Corps of the Karelian Army arrived at the northern tip of Lake Ladoga and continued along the coast to the southeast. The following day 1Lt Aarne Nissinen's pair of 3rd Flight machines surprised two MiG-3s in the Elisenvaara area. One escaped but the other fighter was shot down. Later that same day 1Lt Reino Turkki's swarm of 2nd Flight aircraft were patrolling over Jänisjärvi when they engaged three fighters escorting two DB-3 bombers. While two MS.406s occupied the fighters, the other pair shot down both bombers. One of the pilots to achieve success was future ace 1Lt Pauli Massinen, who claimed his first victory of the Continuation War.

The VII Army Corps of the Karelian Army reached Säämäjärvi – its intermediate target – on 23 July, at which point Commander-in-Chief (C-in-C) Marshal Gustaf Mannerheim called the advance to a halt. The next day the VI Army Corps of the Karelian Army reached its intermediate target of the Tuulosjoki line by Lake Ladoga, and stopped.

That same day, during a reconnaissance mission to Kuusjärvi, 2/LLv 28, led by 1Lt Reino Turkki, engaged three SB bombers of 72nd SBAP. Two were shot down by Sgt Lehtovaara, who recalled;

'When returning from Mangna at 1915 hrs, flying at 2000 m [6500 ft], we met three DB-3 bombers. I attacked the right wing aeroplane and, after firing one burst, it instantly caught fire and crashed.

'The centre aeroplane, with the undercarriage partly down, was shot at by somebody else without any results. When the attacker pulled away behind the middle aeroplane, I immediately moved behind it and fired a burst, and I observed my cannon shells explode behind the starboard engine and fuselage. The aircraft went into a slide and bellied in on a field. Judging by the rate of fire, the dorsal gunner in the second bomber had a heavy-calibre machine gun or cannon.

'My aeroplane was MS314.'

On 12 August a swarm of 1/LLv 28 was engaged in combat over Vieljärvi with six Polikarpov I-15s. One was shot down by 2Lt Linnamaa and another fell after a mid-air collision. This was an I-15bis piloted by Lt V P Gordjun of 65th ShAP, who bailed out. All of the Moranes returned to their base, but MS-301, flown by MSgt Jorma Norola, suffered a smashed starboard wingtip.

Five days later 1Lt Reino Turkki's swarm from 2/LLv 28 was patrolling the Lahdenpohja area when it engaged two I-16s, one of which was shot down by Lehtovaara. The swarm then headed to Lake Ladoga, where two Beriev MBR-2 flying boats were seen taking off in the shelter of Soviet warships. The Moranes remained circling further off until the flying boats had cleared the protection

Pilots of 1/LLv 28 at Läskelä forward landing ground in August 1941. They are, from left to right, SSgt Antti Tani, 2Lt Aarre Linnamaa. 1Lt Aarne Alitalo and MSgt Jaakko Norola. Tani and Linnamaa became aces early the following year, while Norola switched to flying bombers after claiming two victories. Alitalo was the father figure of the squadron (*SA-kuva*)

MS-601 of 3/LLv 28 on the sandy beach at Joensuu in July 1941. Flak brought this aircraft down on 10 August 1941, killing the assigned pilot, 2Lt Reino Ilmonen. Its tactical number was a yellow 0 simply because the standard practice dictated that the tenth aircraft of the flight was so marked (*Finnish Air Force Museum*)

of the naval vessels, after which the swarm attacked and downed them both in flames.

On 20 August 1Lt Reino Valli's reconnaissance swarm of 3/LLv 28 engaged five I-153 *Chaikas* over Rantalahti. In the ensuing combat the Russians had two aircraft shot down, one by Sgt Toivo Tomminen flying MS318.

The following day, over Maaselkä, a swarm from 2/LLv 28 attacked six SB bombers escorted by two I-16s. One of the Tupolevs was destroyed by 1Lt Massinen. Several hours later Capt Urho Nieminen of 3/LLv 26, flying a Buffalo, led a three-aircraft Morane patrol of 1/LLv 28 to Suojärvi, where nine I-15bis were striking Finnish positions. The Finns attacked and the strength of the Russian detachment was decreased by two. The remaining Soviet fighters were then engaged in combat by a pair of 2/LLv 28 aircraft that had appeared on the scene, and the Russians lost one more aircraft.

No more victories were claimed by the Morane unit until 2 September, when 1Lt Tuomo Hyrkki's swarm from 1/LLv 28 flew to Säämäjärvi to protect ground forces. When six I-16s appeared on the scene, the Finnish pilots quickly despatched three of them, Hyrkki reporting;

'On patrol between 1345 hrs and 1520 hrs. When the swarm attacked five I-16s from ahead and above via a half-roll, one fled straight to the east. The I-16 pilot pulled up and turned every now and then, and we fired simultaneously. I caused the engine to smoke, and the aeroplane made a forced landing in a swamp north of Suojujoki. The combat occurred at 50-300 m [160-980 ft] and the I-16 tried to flee at low level. The pilot made a safe forced landing.

MS314 of 2/LLv 28 was photographed at the Karkunranta shore base at Lake Ladoga in September 1941. Its regular pilot was MS.406 ace 1Lt Pauli Massinen, who claimed his first victory in the Winter War. He raised his final tally to five in this very machine on 21 August 1941 when he downed an SB. The aircraft in Massinen's flight had red spinners and white tail numbers (*Pauli Massinen*)

1Lt Pauli Massinen, deputy leader of 2/LLv 28, checks the instruments in the cockpit of his Morane prior to flying his next mission. Massinen's final score of five included four bombers and one flying boat. Having served as an instructor before the Continuation War, Massinen reverted to this role after completing a tour with 2/LLv 28 on 7 November 1941 (*Pauli Massinen*)

Victorious pilots of 2/LLv 28 at Karkunranta on 9 September 1941. They are, from left to right, 2Lt Lasse Lehtonen, Sgt Urho Jääskeläinen, 2Lt Martti Inehmo and SSgt Urho Lehtovaara. On this day Lehtovaara, flying MS-304, claimed three I-16s to boost his overall score to ten. Parked behind the pilots is MS.406 MS-606, which was the assigned aircraft of flight leader 1Lt Reino Turkki (*SA-kuva*)

'My aeroplane was MS-607.'

On 3 September the Karelian Army began the advance from Tuulosjoki towards the River Svir, reaching its objective on the morning of 7 September. In the south the Germans advanced to the southern tip of Lake Ladoga, besieging Leningrad.

Two days later a Morane swarm from 2/LLv 28 engaged nine *Chaikas* and nine I-16bis of 155th IAP during a combat air patrol to the River Svir, shooting six of them down. On the return leg of the mission the detachment encountered an eight-aeroplane mixed formation and destroyed an I-153. SSgt Urho Lehtovaara described his triple claim from the sortie;

'After arriving at the specified area, led by 2Lt Inehmo, we encountered at 1000 hrs nine I-153 and nine I-16bis fighters. Two I-16bis attacked the rearmost pair of the swarm, firing from straight behind. I made an attack from straight ahead against these two, shooting from ahead at the aircraft on the left, which took hits in its engine, made a rapid pull-up and went down in a shallow dive and disappeared with the engine smoking badly. I immediately shot at another I-16bis from straight ahead – it was hit by a long burst and crashed directly into the ground.

'Behind these aeroplanes there was still a three-fighter patrol, which I engaged in a turning fight and managed to shoot at one that was banking, and which crashed at high speed into the forest. One of the remaining aircraft went down to the deck and broke off the fight, and the other pulled into the clouds.

'My aeroplane was MS-304.'

Near Pyhäjärvi on the morning of 12 September 2Lt Aarre Linnamaa's swarm from 1/LLv 28 engaged five 'DB-3' bombers heading towards Prääshä. Three of them were shot down and one was damaged. Linnamaa's combat report stated;

'On patrol between 0710-0830 hrs. Our three-aeroplane patrol met five DBs over Pyhäjärvi en route

SSgt Urho Lehtovaara (right) of 2/LLv 28 poses in front of his assigned aircraft, MS327, at Karkunranta on 9 September 1941 after gaining his tenth kill. Standing alongside the ace is Jukka Paajanen, the fighter's assigned mechanic. Later, when flying Bf 109Gs, Lehtovaara was awarded the Mannerheim Cross after his score exceeded 40 victories (*Pauli Massinen*)

69

THE WINTER WAR

MS-308 of 1/LLv 28 was also photographed at Joensuu in July 1941. Its assigned pilot was 2Lt Aarre Linnamaa, who had already scored one kill in the Winter War, and added a further five in the early stages of the Continuation War. On 5 September 1941 MS-308 was so badly damaged during an air raid on Lunkula that it had to be sent to the State Aircraft Factory to be repaired (*Author's collection*)

to bomb in the direction of Prääshä, altitude 3000 m [9800 ft]. I shot one of the two rearmost aircraft into smoke and flames. It went down burning and on its back.

'We continued our attack against the other aircraft, which pressed down on the deck. We shot at it as we had with the previous aircraft. Then the other three DBs came to our side and I moved behind their tails. Then 2Lt Myllylä and SSgt Tani brought down their aircraft, probably in the Lohijärvi area. I climbed a bit and waved to the boys, but they did not notice and turned away.

'At the same time about ten I-153s were coming towards them at low level. They did not notice me, and I continued after the three DBs. I got one to emit smoke, then another one came by my side. I also made this smoke, expending all of my ammunition. I pulled to the side and observed that the aeroplane at which I had first fired was smoking, and one undercarriage leg was down. The other aeroplane began to smoke heavily. It banked towards the shore of Lake Onega and bellied down into a swamp in the Soksu area. The others continued to fly east-southeast over Lake Onega. On the return flight I encountered a flying boat at Bubnova.

'I got four or five holes in my aircraft. One went through an attachment point of the fuselage tube.

'My aeroplane was MS-607.'

Recently opened Russian archives reveal that the shot-down bombers were in fact three SBs from 72nd SBAP.

This machine, MS-317 of 1/LLv 28, seen at Lunkula in September 1941, was assigned to 2Lt Paavo Myllylä. By the end of 1941 Myllylä's score with this aircraft stood at 1.5 confirmed aerial victories and two probables. Later, flying the Bf 109G, he increased his total to 22 victories (*Finnish Air Force*)

On 15 September 2Lt Paavo Myllylä's swarm from 1/LLv 28 was engaged in a combat with a bomber escorted by five MiG-3 fighters of 179th IAP in the direction of Prääsä. The Moranes shot three of the fighters down, two falling to the guns of 2Lt Paavo Reinikainen;

'On patrol between 1620 hrs and 1735 hrs. We flew in a swarm from Sotjärvi to Prääshä, when one Bis [*sic*] attacked me from ahead and below. I did not see it, but those

coming behind me attacked it. 2Lt Myllylä attacked one DB bomber. Then I saw three fighters and, immediately after, two more, which I attacked. I was at 1500 m [4900 ft] altitude and the enemy at about 300 m [980 ft]. I pressed into a dive after the two fighters and called over my radio for the others to join me. The transmitter was out of order, so they did not hear.

'The aircraft in front of me started to shoot at horse and truck columns. The rearmost Bis dropped four bombs across the road. Soon after this I got it in the sights and shot past it from too far behind. The second burst hit the fuselage behind the pilot. Then I got straight behind, but I was aiming directly at the troops and I could not fire.

'During the pull-up I got the Bis in my sights, but then the aeroplane that was further ahead came towards me and I turned against it and fired a short burst with the machine gun from ahead. The Bis was crosswise in front of me and I turned back to it. The one coming towards me passed 50 m [55 yds] to the right and then I saw that it was not a Bis, as it had an in-line engine and enclosed cockpit. Right after passing me it flipped into a spin and crashed, catching fire. I held the Bis in my sight and managed to shoot from straight behind, but then the cannon jammed and I pulled aside when it broke off straight to the east. The aeroplane did not smoke or slow down, but it took 20 mm hits in the rear fuselage.

'The Russian aeroplanes had good camouflage – no insignias on their uppersurfaces and an uneven spot on the fuselage side.

'My aeroplane was MS-317.'

On 1 October the VII Army Corps of the Karelian Army occupied Petrozavodsk and continued to advance northwards along the west coast of Lake Onega, aiming at Karhumäki at the northern tip of the lake. LLv 28 was flying top cover.

Over Suopohja on 9 October a pair of MS.406s of 2/LLv 28 jumped a climbing detachment of six MiG-3s. When the combat started another pair of Moranes arrived, and all of the Russian fighters were shot down. 2Lt Martti Ihehmo claimed two destroyed and one damaged;

'We flew about eight kilometres [five miles] north to Suopohja, and I observed at 1115 hrs an enemy fighter climbing in the direction of Suopohja. I gained altitude and attacked from straight ahead, but I had to pull aside. More enemy aircraft were taking off all the time, and at one point I observed at least five I-18s [MiG-3s]. In the ensuing turning fight

MS315 and MS329 of 3/LLv 28 at Solomanni in October 1941. The former was flown by SSgt Oskari Jussila and the latter by Sgt Toivo Tomminen. Jussila claimed four victories and Tomminen 6.5, all in Moranes in both cases. Tomminen died on 4 December 1941 when he was rammed head-on in MS329 by 2Lt N F Repnikov in 152nd IAP Hurricane IIB BD761 (*Author's collection*)

MS327 of 2/LLv 28, seen here at Viitana in eastern Karelia in December 1941, was assigned to MSgt Urho Lehtovaara, the top-scoring MS.406 pilot with 14 confirmed aerial victories. On 23 December 1941 MS327 caught fire during a warming-up procedure and was destroyed (*Pauli Massinen*)

I shot one directly from behind at 20-30 m [20-30 yds] distance. I saw the cannon shells hit its fuselage, which promptly puffed thick smoke and the aircraft jerked up, going right into a cloud. I began turning, and saw it come out of the cloud, but I was instantly attacked by another fighter. I continued the turning fight with it and after a while another I-18 joined in. They tried to cut off my exit to the west, and I ended up doing evasive manoeuvres all the way to Soralahti, where I managed to shoot at one from straight ahead. It then pulled up and went into a dive, crashing in the water near an island.

'I continued the turning fight with the other I-18 at 600 m [2000ft] at first, but it forced me below 100 m [300 ft]. Finally, I managed to get in a deflection shot from left below and behind, after which it banked, smoking, and crashed into the forest, where it exploded and caught fire.

'My aeroplane was MS327.'

On 19 October 1Lt Aarne Nissinen's swarm of 3/LLv 28 flew a search to Poventsa and engaged a Polikarpov R-Z reconnaissance biplane, which was sent down. Two *Chaikas* appeared on the scene and both were shot down as well. Two of the enemy aircraft were credited to Sgt Toivo Tomminen;

'Between 1310-1320 hrs I observed an R-Z heading towards Poventsa. I dived after it and fired one burst, after which both port wings broke off and the aeroplane crashed into a lake. Then I saw two I-153s taking off from Poventsa airfield. I attacked the rearmost as soon as it had left the ground. I fired a burst from behind and it crashed into a field on its nose. I had obviously hit the pilot.

'While I was shooting at the I-153, pieces of it flew off. A section of plating hit my starboard wing and stuck in it. There was no other damage.

'My aeroplane was MS315.'

Soon wintry weather began to set in, and poor weather and heavy snowfall prevented much flying on both sides. Only two victories were claimed by the Moranes during November.

On 4 December a swarm from 3/LLv 28 was engaged in combat by three 'I-18s' (MiG-3s) over Maaselkä. Both sides lost one aircraft in a mid-air collision. One of the participants was SSgt Pekka Vassinen;

'At 1300-1305 hrs, as we approached Maaselkä from the southwest at 1000 m [3300 ft] – I was flying on the left wing and about 400 m [440 yds] to the side – I observed two [I-18s] climbing from below and behind at an angle of about 45 degrees. The enemy still had a considerable speed advantage at our altitude.

'Sgt Tomminen had also observed one I-18, which was shooting at SSgt Jussila from 100 m [100 yds] behind. Sgt Tomminen shot at the I-18 from the side, getting hits from behind the engine to the cockpit. The I-18 suddenly pulled up, and Sgt Tomminen hit the wing of the I-18, snapping it off. Sgt Tomminen's aeroplane flipped onto its back, flew a while in this position and then its nose slowly sank into a vertical dive. A moment later I saw the aircraft burning on the ground. I descended to ground level, but did not see any parachutes. The aircraft shot at by Sgt Tomminen crashed in flames.

'The rate of climb of the I-18 was obviously good, because some time earlier Sgt Tomminen had been down at low level and not seen anything. The Russians opened fire from relatively close range.

'My aeroplane was MS-620.'

The war diary of 152nd IAP, flying Hurricanes, noted;

'Between 1255 hrs and 1410 hrs (Moscow time) three aircraft carried out a reconnaissance of enemy positions in the areas of railway junction No 13, Medvezhjegorsk, Par-guba, Kamselga, Kumsa and west of Pokrov. The mission was accomplished. The aircraft were then engaged in a combat two kilometres [one mile] south of Kriv with seven Heinkels and Me 109s. The result of the battle was two enemy fighters shot down. Additionally, 1Lt N F Repnikov rammed one Me 109 from straight ahead, our pilot being killed.'

Although the regimental war diary identifies the enemy aircraft as 'Heinkels and Me 109's', in the claim list of 152nd IAP these three kills appeared as 'Brewsters', one of which Lts Basov and Lt S Ivanov reported sharing. The other aircraft involved in the collision was clearly MS.406 MS-329, but otherwise the details of the reports do not quite match.

The fin of MS318 of 2/LLv 28, seen at Viitana in November 1941, displays bars denoting the eight victories of 2Lt Martti Inehmo – the final tally of the second-highest scoring Finnish MS.406 ace. Inehmo failed to return from a mission on Boxing Day 1941, when he was flying MS-618 (*Jaakko Puolakkainen*)

STALEMATE WAR

On Finnish independence day, 6 December, the last point reached by the advancing Karelian Army was the town of Poventsa, which was occupied. Marshal Mannerheim then called a halt to the offensive, and two-and-a-half years of stalemate duly followed. Except for a few local clashes, the whole frontline fell silent. In LLv 28's sector (Lake Onega and Maaselkä Isthmus) the airspace was just as quiet. In the air, Soviet and Finnish forces were quantitatively rather even, although the *Ilmavoimat* still possessed a qualitative advantage.

On 5 February 1942 a Morane swarm from 1/LLv 28, led by 2Lt Aarre Linnamaa, flew a reconnaissance mission to Osta at the eastern end of the River Svir. En route, two Polikarpov R-5 reconnaissance biplanes were met and shot down, as Linnamaa relates;

'Between 0945 hrs and 0950 hrs, at an altitude of 10-20 m [30-65 ft], I was leading a four-aeroplane swarm along the river valley southwest from Androvkaya, shooting at trucks, when I saw an R-5 flying to the southwest in the surface fog in the valley. MSgt Tani initially fired at it from above me, but he probably did not hit it because the biplane continued as before. I then fired at it in a surprise attack from a distance of 70 m [75 yds] down to 15 m [20 yds] from above and behind. The aeroplane glided towards the ice on the river, whereupon two more aircraft shot at it, although it was already unable to fly. The aeroplane hit the ice hard (the pilot was probably dead) and turned over onto its back.

'I continued to the southwest and encountered another R-5 in the same valley as the previous one. I fired first from the side and soon after that from behind at 20 m [22 yds], and the biplane dived into the forest and flipped onto its side, at which point Capt Blomqvist shot at it from a distance, although the aircraft had already disappeared into the forest.

'I did not see any men leave the first aeroplane. The second one broke up into pieces upon hitting the forest. I did not observe the gunners firing at me.

'My aeroplane was MS-621.'

On 23 March two Moranes of 1/LLv 28 were scrambled when a pair of Petlyakov Pe-2 bombers attacked Petrozavodsk. They managed to shoot

MS-325 and MS328 of 1/LLv 28 are ready for take-off at Viitana on 17 March 1942. Two weeks after this photograph was taken MS-325 was assigned to the new flight leader, Capt Pekka Siiriäinen, and MS328 was assigned to Capt Tuomo Hyrkki. The latter machine is still painted in French camouflage (*SA-kuva*)

one of the aircraft down, as MSgt Antti Tani reported;

'After an earlier test flight in MS-619 I took off in this aircraft directly from the blast pen. At 0825 hrs, when I had reached an altitude of 1500 m [4900 ft], I received a radio message – two Pe-2s from Soksu heading directly north. I was then in a steep climb heading directly for Äänislinna, and at the same time I climbed through the clouds. Then I made a 360-degree climbing turn,

Seen at Viitana on 17 March 1942, MS-607 of 1/LLv 28 was 2Lt Aarre Linnamaa's second assigned aeroplane, in which he scored two of his six victories with Moranes. He was killed on 24 April 1942 after making a forced landing in enemy territory (*SA-kuva*)

after which I observed the enemy aeroplane about two kilometres [one mile] away and 300-500 m [1000-1600 ft] higher than me.

'When the distance had reduced to 250-300 m [800-1000ft] I fired, but the deflection was too small. I pulled more deflection, fired and again increased the deflection. Now the burst seemed to hit. After this I turned behind the aeroplane at 300-400 m [330-430 yds] and fired three bursts. After the last one the aeroplane made a steep 180-degree turn and began a shallow ascent. It appeared to me that the bomber had lost considerable speed. I tried to fire again, but my Colt guns jammed.

'While I was fixing this problem the aeroplane made a steep 90-degree turn towards me, and I dodged with a combat Immelmann turn. During that manoeuvre my guns began to work again, and at the moment of passing I observed that the enemy aeroplane had fallen into a spin. Then it seemed that the pilot cut the engines. I thought this was a bluff, so I followed the aeroplane down in a spiral from a position some 800-1000 m [2600-3300 ft] higher, waiting for it to level off. When the aeroplane reached 300-500 m [1000-1600 ft] altitude I knew that it could no longer pull up. The bomber hit the ground right after that.'

By 3 May 1942 the fronts had remained calm for six months. The air arm took advantage of this lull in the action to reorganise itself, with the control of frontline units being divided up along territorial lines. This change was heavily criticised by the leaders of the

Allocated to long-time flight leader 1Lt Reino Turkki, MS-606 of 2/LLv 28 is seen at Viitana in March 1942. Almost an ace, Turkki was credited with four confirmed kills and two probables. He later rose to the rank of lieutenant general and became the commander of the *Ilmavoimat* in 1964 (*Finnish Air Force Museum*)

The deputy leader of 3/LLv 28, 1Lt Jouko Myllymäki (left), and SSgt Pekka Vassinen brief in front of MS-616 at Solomanni on 23 March 1942. Myllymäki scored two victories on Moranes and later became an ace after adding three kills while flying the Bf 109G-2. His was listed as missing in action on 25 June 1944 (*SA-kuva*)

MSgt Urho Lehtovaara runs the engine up in MS-304 of 3/LLv 28 on Petrozavodsk airfield, Solomanni, on 26 March 1942. Although the aeroplane did not have a tactical number, it was marked with six bars denoting the victories that had been achieved in MS-304 by various pilots – three of them by Lehtovaara on 9 September 1941. He would claim another kill in this aircraft on 4 April 1942 (*SA-kuva*)

fighter regiments, however, as they believed that in the new system the most important feature of the air arm, mobility, could not be fully exploited.

Despite the reorganisation, LeR 2 continued to operate with the Maaselkä Group. In addition to LeLv 24 and LeLv 28 (the squadron abbreviation had changed from LLv to LeLv during the reorganisation), LeR 2 also added LeLv 16 to its ranks. In the regiment's new sector of responsibility its territorial limit to the left was set at Lieksanjärvi-Kuusiniemi-Vojatsu-Virma and to the right at Lohijärvi-Derevjannoje-Ääninen-Volodarskaja-Vytegra.

LeR 2's tasks were specified as 1) reconnaissance, artillery, bombing and transport missions, 2) interception of enemy aircraft and 3) protection of transports, transfer flights and bombers. These missions were to be flown at the request of the Maaselkä Group, the Onega Coastal Brigade and the Olonets Group. In practice LeLv 16 reconnoitred the closer areas at Maaselkä, LeLv 24 took care of interception and long-range reconnaissance along the whole front and LeLv 28 was responsible for Lake Onega and the areas south of it.

On 3 August LeLv 28 became LeR 2's sole fighter unit, and its sector was extended to the Maaselkä Isthmus. The HQ and the 3rd Flight of the squadron moved to Hirvas and the 1st Flight was sent to Petrozavodsk.

Several weeks earlier a 700-man Soviet partisan brigade had slipped through the lines undetected east of Lake Ontajärvi, and by the end of July it had managed to advance to a position 40 km (25 miles) southwest of

MS328 of 1/LeLv 28, seen at Solomanni in May 1942, was assigned to flight leader Capt Tuomo Hyrkki. For many years officially credited with four confirmed victories whilst flying the MS.406, Hyrkki recently 'made ace' when his claim for an I-16 damaged on 8 June 1943 was upgraded to destroyed following information gleaned from the Russian archives (*Author's collection*)

Lake Segozero, into the rear of the Maaselkä Group. Once engaged by the Finnish Army, the partisans retreated along the same route – its remaining troops crossed the waterways at Lake Jolmozero. On 18 August a swarm of 1/LeLv 28 MS.406s was sent to Jolmozero to strafe the partisans crossing the waterways. The troops were protected by a four-Hurricane detachment, of which the Moranes shot one down and damaged two more. As SSgt Matti Leinonen reported;

'On patrol between 0740 hrs and 0900 hrs, flying mainly at an altitude of 600 m [2000 ft]. While the swarm was strafing the enemy's transport barges at Jolmozero, four Hurricanes attacked us. I managed to shoot the first one obliquely from behind, whereupon it started to smoke heavily. At the same time another came obliquely towards me, and I also fired at this aircraft. It broke off, smoking, and disappeared down to low level. I followed the first one, firing short bursts all the time. The aeroplane staggered and flew out of control, constantly losing altitude and speed. It then flew along a swamp valley at a height of just 5-6 m [16-20 ft], the terrain rising to the east. The speed of the aeroplane was then so low that my MS.406 could not stay behind the enemy fighter, and I tended to pass it. The Hurricane pilots were not willing to fire from straight ahead, dodging in time to avoid fire and attempting to approach from below and behind. I received no damage.

'My aeroplane was MS-619.'

On a later mission that same day eight Moranes patrolling over Jolmozero were attacked by a similar number of Tomahawks. One Soviet fighter was damaged, but a Morane was shot down. Russian records reveal that the Hurricanes and Tomahawks of 152nd IAP and 195th IAP reported having shot down four Fokkers and one Brewster in the Maaselkä area – quite an escalation from the loss of one Morane.

On 24 August Maj Auvo Maunula took over the command of LeLv 28. Two weeks later he was awarded the Mannerheim Cross for earlier achievements as the commander of a reconnaissance squadron.

MS-619 of 1/LeLv 28 at Petrozavodsk, Solomanni, in August 1942. It was assigned to MSgt Antti Tani, who claimed seven kills with Moranes out of his total of 20.5 confirmed victories. Unusually, the fighter's tactical number is present in white outline form only (*Author's collection*)

MS-622 of 2/LeLv 28 has been hoisted onto supports at Hirvas for undercarriage testing following a nose-up landing on 22 October 1942. The aircraft escaped without incurring any serious damage. It was regularly flown during this period by Sgt Pentti Piispa (*Finnish Air Force*)

On 1 September three Pe-2s bombed Hirvas airfield in a surprise attack. When the swarm of LeLv 28 Moranes on duty got airborne, 29 Tomahawks, Hurricanes, I-153s and I-15s suddenly appeared from the north and began to strafe the airfield with machine guns. Two MS.406s were scrambled from Solomanni to assist, but they were slow in getting airborne and then faced jamming problems with their heavy weapons once overhead Hirvas. As a result only one Tomahawk was damaged for the loss of a Morane. After the raid a single Pe-2 photographed the target.

The Hurricanes and Tomahawks of 152nd IAP and 195th IAP and the *Chaikas* of 828th ShAP reported having shot down four Brewsters in the Hirvas area, when only a solitary Morane had in fact been lost.

From 16 September Russian air activity increased on the Maaselkä Isthmus, and the pilots and aircraft of LeLv 28, now few in number, began to face difficulties. To improve the situation Detachment Luukkanen, consisting of ten Brewsters from LeLv 24, was transferred to Hirvas and seconded to LeR 2. Within two weeks, however, Russian missions in the Maaselkä area had decreased again owing to units being transferred to the north to escort vital supply convoys bound for Murmansk and Archangel. Detachment Luukkanen of LeLv 24 soon returned to the Karelian Isthmus.

NEW OLD AEROPLANES

On 16 July 1942 Finland bought 30 MS.406s directly from Vichy France. This drew a protest from the Germans, who claimed that the official channels were not used, but nothing more came of it. The aircraft had

MS-624 of 2/LeLv 28, photographed at Hirvas whilst assigned to Sgt Uolevi Jaakkola, was temporarily painted in white winter camouflage on 20 February 1943. The whitewash 'recipe' employed by 2/LeLv 28 groundcrew consisted of casein glue mixed with chalk powder (*Erkki Jaakkola*)

been flown to Finland in three batches by 9 September 1942. The State Aircraft Factory gave them a full overhaul, and they began to reach squadrons in October. The serial numbers for these aircraft were MS-626 to MS-655. In late 1942 the last two Moranes, MS-656 and MS-657, bought from the Germans, were flown to Finland.

There was little aerial activity over the Maaselkä Isthmus during the final months of 1942, however, with the only contacts being a few visual observations along the frontline. This all changed on 12 January 1943 when a swarm of Moranes from 2/LeLv 28 was on an escort and search mission in the Nopsa area. The Finnish fighters engaged four Pe-2 bombers escorted by three Hurricanes, and one of the latter machines was shot down by MSgt Urho Lehtovaara. He reported;

'While patrolling between 1235 and 1445 hrs between Liistepohja and Karhumäki we observed north of Maaselkä at a very high altitude one Pe-2 aircraft, which glittered as it continued to gain altitude. We immediately climbed after it, and after about ten minutes I was in a position to open fire from about 600 m [655 yds] below and behind.

'Simultaneously, a Hurricane fired at me from above and behind, and I had to give up the chase. A turning fight then developed between three Hurricanes and myself. I managed to shoot at one of my opponents in a bank, and scored a hit with the burst, whereupon the Hurricane suddenly stalled and fell away in a spin down to the ground, where it exploded and burned. Right after this I was able to fire at the second Hurricane, which evaded, smoking. The third Hurricane broke off the battle in a dive and disappeared to the northeast.

'My aeroplane was MS-627.'

On 24 February a pair of MS.406s from 1/LeLv 28 encountered a lone Pe-2 over Sautjärvi. After a short pursuit it was sent down by MSgt Antti Tani, who recalled;

'While on an interception mission I was radioed at 1255 hrs about an aeroplane flying southwards from Maasjärvi. I was flying in the same direction, and sighted it after about four minutes. At Tokari the aeroplane turned north. Then I managed to fire from ahead on the right side, when the starboard engine began to smoke, first weakly and then stronger all the time. I followed the aeroplane until it crashed. During the pursuit I fired a further three bursts into it.

MSgt Antti Tani and his mechanic, Risto Hiltunen, at Solomanni in front of 1/LeLv 28 machine MS-619 in March 1943. Tani claimed two Pe-2s destroyed in MS-619 on 25 March 1942 and 24 February 1943. His real haul came with the Bf 109G, when he added 13.5 victories to his tally (*Risto Hiltunen*)

Seen at Hirvas, in eastern Karelia, during March 1943, MS-615 of LeLv 28 was flown by unit CO, Maj Auvo Maunula. He had three victories to his credit, and six months earlier he had been awarded the Mannerheim Cross for his bravery and leadership whilst serving as a reconnaissance pilot and commander. His rank allowed him to use a large blue-and-white 'X' as a tactical marking on his assigned MS.406 (*Author's collection*)

Borrowed by LeLv 34 for a series of evaluation flights, MS328 was photographed at Utti in early 1943. On 5 May 1943 it was returned to 1/LeLv 28 and assigned to Sgt Martti Vihinen. The five victory bars marked on the leading edge of the fighter's fin denote kills by four different pilots. The winter camouflage was typical for most squadron machines during this period (*Klaus Niska collection*)

'My aeroplane was MS-619.'

On 5 March a Morane patrol of 2/LeLv 28 scrambled in pursuit of a bomber northwest of Karhumäki. MSgt Urho Lehtovaara reported thus;

'I took off at 1355 hrs on an alarm mission and climbed to 5000 m [16,400 ft] northwest of Karhumäki. I was radioed that there was one aircraft north of Savujärvi. Immediately below me against the clouds I saw a twin-engined aircraft heading north. I dived after it and soon recognised that it was a Pe-2. I shot at the bomber from directly behind, hitting the starboard engine and setting it on fire. The aeroplane crashed into the ground, where it remained burning. During the dive one man bailed out of the burning aircraft.

'I followed the burning aeroplane down so as to pinpoint the exact location of the crash site, but at an altitude of about 1000 m [3300 ft] I was attacked by four I-16s. I fought a fierce aerial battle with the four enemy aeroplanes. My windscreen had been covered in oil from the Pe-2, and this obstructed my view to such an extent that several of my bursts missed the target. I finally got behind and slightly below one of the enemy fighters and gave it a long burst. Some of the I-16's ventral plating came loose and the aircraft fell away to port and hit the ground. I also tried to fire at the other enemy fighters, which still kept attacking me, but my aircraft's machine guns stopped working, so I was forced to break off the combat.

'My aeroplane was MS-641.'

The CO of 2/LeLv 28, Capt Reino Turkki, and his wingmen intercepted two Hurricanes in the Käppäselkä area on 4 May. One of the Soviet fighters was subsequently claimed as destroyed, as Turkki explained;

'I had scrambled at 0940 hrs with a three-aeroplane patrol, and at Käppäselkä we encountered two Hurricanes at an altitude of 2000 m [6,500 ft]. In the ensuing combat I shot at both aeroplanes. One of the aircraft, with silver-coloured wings, soon broke away from the combat. After this I was harassing the other Hurricane with 2Lt Tarkkonen, shooting at it twice from short range. It started to pour smoke during the turning fight, but the pilot then took evasive action and the speed of the Morane could not match it.

'During the chase I observed an aircraft flying on the deck south of Povents, which I easily caught. It began to smoke heavily after my first burst. After the second burst I suffered a gun malfunction. I followed the aircraft and saw it fall on the east bank of the Voljärvi Canal, strong blue smoke puffing out of its engine. The aeroplane did not burn and the fuselage was clearly visible in the forest.

'The Hurricane is not as agile as the Morane. Flak was fired from Käppäselkä during the combat.

'My aeroplane was MS-626.'

Turkki had engaged three Ilyushin Il-2 ground attack aeroplanes after his clash with the Hurricanes, and as he noted in his combat report, he had been able to shoot one down. Another pilot in his swarm claimed a second Il-2 destroyed.

Four days later a pair of LeLv 28 Moranes that were on a search mission to Seesjärvi were bounced by a detachment of four I-16s. In the ensuing combat two Russian aircraft were sent down immediately and a third a short while later – the fourth I-16 escaped. Leading the Finnish fighters was unit CO Maj Auvo Maunula, who described this action as follows;

'While I was flying a search mission with a patrol I met at 1915 hrs four low-flying I-16s at Suontele – they were about 1500 m [5000 ft] below us. I surprised them as they were shooting at the ground at the time. I chose a target, but when I dived towards it another observed me and began to climb and bank in my direction. I broke off my attack and, after climbing and turning, got above and behind the second I-16.

'The aeroplane quickly evaded by diving away. I went after it, and once the fighter was in my sights I fired a short burst from obliquely behind. I could not see the results because another aeroplane was attacking me from above and to the right. By pulling up I was able to get above it to one side. Then the I-16 commenced a series of rolls, some of which, in a 30-degree dive, approached the deck. I managed to fire a short burst, but then observed two aircraft 300-400 m [1000-1300 ft] above me on the port side.

'By climbing and banking I was able to get above and slightly behind the pair of I-16s just as they commenced a dive from about 1000 m [3300 ft] down to the deck. They headed east, and I followed one aircraft that continued to fly on the deck, easily dodging the short bursts I fired at it. I was struggling with my aim, but eventually the pilot tried to break off by climbing into a banking turn. During this manoeuvre I shot a long burst from a distance of just 100-75 m [110-80 yds], hitting the front fuselage. The aeroplane then dived into a bay below me and disappeared under the sludge.

'My aeroplane was MS-615.'

On 4 June 1Lt Juhani Ruuskanen's Morane pair from 3/LeLv 28 were scrambled to Seesjärvi, where they engaged two SB bombers, both of which were shot down in flames. Ruuskanen reported;

'I took off with 2Lt Antere on an interception mission at 1325 hrs following receipt of an air surveillance message stating that two bombers had been sighted to the southwest at an altitude of 40 m [130 ft]. We spotted the aeroplanes southwest of Semsjärvi as they flew towards us at an altitude of 150 m [490 ft] – we were at 400 m [1300 ft]. They did not see us until we were very close, at which point they immediately turned north. I took the port one for myself and fired at it from 150-100 m [160-110 yds] with three short bursts prior to my guns jamming. After this I saw 2Lt Antere fire at the aeroplanes from 150-100 m distance. I managed to fix my machine guns to fire one round at a time, and when I noticed that Antere's guns had also jammed I switched the control column to my left hand and in turn made cocking manoeuvres with my right hand.

'I had fired about 20 rounds at the aircraft on the right from 50-20 m [55-22 yds] when the centre fuselage caught fire, but the flames were soon blown out again by the slipstream. I shot off a further ten rounds, at which point the bomber caught fire again and crash landed onto Lake Seesjärvi and sank. I then shot two rounds into the port engine of the other aeroplane from about 20 m [22 yds]. It caught fire immediately, the flames spread fast and the aeroplane fell burning into Lake Seesjärvi and sank. The pilot did not try actual low-level flying, instead remaining straight and level all the time. Although his bomber was burning, the nose gunner in the first bomber fired three long bursts into the ground at the tip of a peninsula northeast of Jouhivaara.

'My aeroplane was MS-657.'

Four days later, at noon 1/LeLv 28 leader Capt Tuomo Hyrkki's swarm escorted Fokker C.X dive-bombers of 3/LeLv 16 north of Maaselkä. Over Sumeri railway station they engaged two I-16s. One was shot down and the other escaped due to the malfunctioning of the Moranes' heavy machine guns. Hyrkki's report stated;

'After the FK [Fokker] aeroplanes bombed a train two kilometres [one mile] north of Sumeri railway station, two I-16s appeared on the scene, obviously planning to attack the FKs. I pushed my aeroplane into a dive and bank when the enemy fighters turned towards me. I shot at both from straight ahead, but without any obvious results. I made a fast turn, but ended up too close to the enemy after the turn, so the enemy could not fire at me properly and I could not fire at the enemy aeroplane either.

'After passing it I made a swift turn and ended up in the opposite direction again from the enemy aeroplanes, which were flying in a row about 200 m [220 yds] apart from each other. I got a good bead and opened fire from a distance of about 200 m, and I saw the burst hit the engine. The enemy aeroplane went into a dive and soon after that it caught fire. The pilot bailed out.

'I managed to shoot at the other one twice from relatively close range, but due to gun malfunctions I was forced to break off the combat. At one point black smoke came out of the enemy aeroplane, but it stopped before I had to leave the battle. The enemy aircraft were using rocket projectiles, which after being fired from the wings exploded 50-10 m [55-11 yds] behind the aircraft!

'My aeroplane was MS-657.'

Recent research in the Russian archives proved that both of the I-16s, from 197th IAP, were shot down. Thus Hyrkki gained his fourth and fifth victories, and 'acedom'.

On 16 June the long-time commander of LeR 2, Col Richard Lorentz, was transferred to the air force headquarters as the inspector of air warfare, and Lt Col Raoul Harju-Jeanty was appointed as his successor. The new CO's first job was to specify the tasks of the regiment as follows – LeLv 16

MS-611 of 1/LeLv 14 at Tiiksjärvi in
March 1943. Sgt Aaro Nuorala, who
was the fighter's regular pilot, scored
1.5 victories with the Morane, and
ended the war with 14.5 victories to
his credit. 1/LeLv 14 applied white
tail numbers to its MS.406s, 18 being
the highest known (*Kaarlo Temmes*)

was in charge of the reconnaissance of enemy shipping and ports in Lake
Onega, photography of the mouths of the Vodla and Vyterga rivers, and
bombing of the ports, piers and warehouses at Tsolmutsa, on the Vodla
river, and at Vytegra. LeLv 28 was to escort LeLv 16 assets when necessary,
in addition to conducting its interception duties.

Three days later the commander of the *Ilmavoimat* instructed LeR 2 to
save fuel, and it in turn told LeLv 28 that the unit was only permitted to
take off to intercept enemy aircraft or escort Finnish machines on the
direct orders of LeR 2's commander. The already quiet Lake Onega sector
grew even quieter, and only one minor and inconclusive clash occurred
in the latter half of 1943.

SOUTH VIENA FRONT

LeLv 14, stationed on the northernmost airfield at Tiiksjärvi, close to the
White Sea, was reorganised on 1 August 1942. The 1st Flight had begun
receiving MS.406s as their sole equipment, and the pilots transferred to
the flight had previously flown Fokker D.XXIs in the reconnaissance and
interception roles. The Moranes would take over the fighter duties, as well
as the more demanding reconnaissance missions.

On 1 September LeLv 14 flew its first mission with the Moranes, while
training and evaluation was still in progress. By November the flight was
fully operational and in charge of the airspace. The unit had to wait until
5 November, however, to claim its first victory. On that date a pair of
Moranes from 1/LeLv 14, led by 1Lt Martti Kalima, flew a reconnaissance
mission to Segozero, where they were bounced by a single LaGG-3.
Another LaGG soon appeared on the scene and both were sent down.
Since five more Russian fighters were seen approaching, the Finns decided
to break off and return to Tiiksjärvi. The squadron's first Morane victory
is recounted here by Kalima;

'Between 1155 hrs and 1340 hrs I patrolled with Sgt Leino at an
altitude of 2500 m [8200 ft] west of Voijärvi, heading eastwards. From
the north came one LaGG-3 flying almost on the wing of Leino, who was
on my right and about 200 m [650 ft] below. Leino tried to get behind
the LaGG, but it dodged towards me in a climbing turn. The pilot

The two victory bars adorning the rudder of MS-319 of 1/LeLv 14 at Tiiksjärvi in the summer of 1943 denote the I-152 kills gained by Sgt Hemmo Leino on 16 March that year. Leino had three Morane claims in his final tally of 11 confirmed victories (*Toivo Vuorinen*)

obviously failed to see me, so I easily got behind it. The fighter pulled into a shallow dive to the east and tried to escape. I was about 100 m [110 yds] away from it, took a glimpse in the rear mirror and saw the nose of an enemy aircraft behind me, and at the same time a burst passed over me. I planned to evade, but the aeroplane in the mirror then flipped to starboard and emitted black smoke. I took aim again on the one ahead of me and fired a short burst. Pieces tore off behind the cockpit and the aeroplane pulled slightly up, banking to the starboard side. I fired at it from 60 m [65 yds] and the aeroplane burst into flames and went down in a spin.

'The enemy fighters had smoke tracers, and appeared to be clumsily flown. There was no damage to my MS-326.'

Kalima also became an ace on this mission, and continued claiming to become the unit's top scorer, and evidently its only MS.406 ace.

Generally, the chances for scoring aerial victories on this front were scarce, as there was little aerial activity over South Viena through to the end of hostilities in September 1944. Occasionally, however, something happened. For example, on 14 March 1943 a Finnish commando detachment commenced the destruction of Russian partisan stores in Jeljärvi village. For the next two days LeLv 14 flew top cover for the vehicular transport carrying the detachment along the Rukajärvi-Ontajärvi road. In addition, a six-aeroplane Morane detachment from LeLv 28 flew from Tiiksjärvi for four days to provide top cover during the destruction of the Jeljärvi warehouses.

On 16 March the commandos destroyed the stores at Jeljärvi free from Russian aerial interference. Shortly after that the five Moranes of 2/LeLv 28 escorting the commandos shot down two Tomahawks from a formation of five. One of the fighters was claimed by SSgt Vesa Janhonen;

'When patrolling between 1145 and 1350 hrs south of Jeljärvi I observed SSgt Jussila pull up and bank to the right, where I noticed five aircraft, of which four attacked, trying to get in behind our swarm. We were then 200 m [650 ft] lower than the attackers. We dodged the enemy fighters by banking. After this the clash became a turning fight. I observed one enemy behind 1Lt Ala-Panula. I attacked from about 300 m [980 ft] above the Tomahawk, firing at it from behind and below from a distance of 50-60 m [55-65 yds]. I had to dodge another enemy machine, so I could not see the results of my shooting.

'After this I was subjected to several attacks, which I again dodged by banking. The enemy aircraft now began a turning fight, after which it pulled up – I could not follow it in the pull-up. I began to climb after it, and as I was about to get behind its tail it turned into a dive and began heading to the southeast, away from the scene of the combat. I went after the Tomahawk at full throttle and got to within 100 m [110 yds] of it

MS-311 of 1/LeLv 14 at Tiiksjärvi, in south Viena, on 20 June 1943. This machine was often flown by 2Lt Lasse Kurten. Although it was not an 'ace' aeroplane, MS-311 had the distinction of sporting a 'sharksmouth' for a short period in the summer of 1943 (*Author's collection*)

before firing from straight behind. The enemy began to bank to the right. I shot at it as it banked, and the fighter crashed in the forest.

'In the final stages of the combat we were down on the deck. I chased another Tomahawk, which appeared on the wing of the second machine I was firing at without helping his comrade in any way to break off. I crossed the Murmansk railway behind it and gave up the chase, not being able to catch it. My aeroplane, MS-645, suffered no damage.'

Throughout that day LeLv 14 undertook 35 sorties. In the afternoon Capt Martti Tainio's Morane flight managed to surprise a ten-aircraft I-15bis detachment from 839th IAP, sending five down on their first pass and a further two during the ensuing combat. Future ace Sgt Hemmo Leino claimed two aerial victories, and his combat report briefly stated;

'Between 1425 hrs and 1435 hrs over Jeljärvi-Kotskoma at an altitude of 50 m [160 ft] I observed three I-15s heading east below me. I attacked the lead aeroplane and shot at it until it fell into the forest. After this the wingmen banked away, and now I began shooting at the aircraft flying on the starboard side. It caught fire, but the fire went out, after which it rolled onto its back and disappeared from my sight since I had to pull up to avoid a collision.

'My aeroplane was MS-319.'

Exactly one week after commandos attacked the Jeljärvi store a Morane pair from 1/LeLv 14, led by 1Lt Martti Kalima, shot down an I-16 east of Lake Ontajarvi. Kalima reported;

'At 0840-0845 hrs, flying at an altitude of 200 m [660 ft] with Sgt Nuorala, I met two eastbound I-16bis aeroplanes east of Lake Ontajärvi. We managed to take them by surprise from behind, and when closing in (distance 50-70 m [55-75 yds]) I fired at the aeroplane on the port wing, which burst into flames and evaded, but the fire went out. Early in the turning fight Sgt Nuorala and I got behind the I-16bis and we both fired bursts at short range, causing the aircraft to catch fire and crash.

'My aeroplane was MS-326.'

The following months were quiet both in the air and on the ground on the South Viena Front. Enemy aircraft were occasionally seen, but they avoided contact.

On 14 February 1944 the squadrons at the front were renamed according to their function. Since LeLv 14 was basically a reconnaissance squadron, its new abbreviation was TLeLv 14.

On 13 April the Morane swarm of 2/TLeLv 14 leader Capt Martti Kalima went to Rukajärvi for an interception. They met two LaGG-3s, one of which was shot down. The other pilot used his aircraft's speed to escape. The unit's next aerial action occurred on 26 May when 2/TLeLv 14, led by Capt Kalima, was on a reconnaissance mission to Jeljärvi and it engaged four LaGG-3s. They tried to break off, but one of them failed to do so in time and fell prey to Finnish guns.

One week later Morane pairs from 1/ and 2/TLeLv 14 reconnoitred Kuutsjärvi, where they encountered ten LaGGs. One Morane was hit but managed to return to Tiiksjärvi. The Russians, on the other hand, lost three aircraft. Capt Martti Kalima, who shot down two of them, wrote;

'Patrolled Kuutsjärvi-Ontajärvi from 1500 m down to 50m [4900 ft to 165 ft] between 1750 hrs and 1900 hrs. I was top-cover leader on a reconnaissance mission when four LaGG-3s attacked us at Jeljärvi, two going for the low patrol and two for my patrol. In the ensuing turning fight I fought two Russians after some fighters that joined the fray forced my wingman away from me. After the initial pass, both Russians circled at an altitude of 1000 m [3330 ft]. I surprised one and got at its neck from above, zooming up and bouncing it. After my fourth such pass the aeroplane spun away and crashed into the forest.

Capt Martti Kalima, flight leader of 2/TLeLv 14, in front of his Morane, MS-622, at Tiiksjärvi in early June 1944. Kalima was his unit's only MS.406 ace, with 6.5 kills bringing his score to 11 in total. All of his earlier successes had been achieved flying Twin Wasp-engined Fokker D.XXIs in 1941 (*Ragnar Rosenberg*)

'After this I gained altitude because I saw three more enemy aeroplanes coming in from the southwest some 500 m [1600 ft] higher than me. My wingman, Capt Anttonen, then attacked the solitary enemy whose wingman I had just shot down. I was in a shallow rising turn when, out of the sun, two more aeroplanes attacked me. I was slow to evade and I was hit in the wing and my undercarriage dropped down. I tried to break off into a cloud but did not make it, and I had to go down on the deck instead. We fought on at treetop height, and I wound up some 12-15 km [7-9 miles] southwest of Ontajärvi. Finally, I had no choice but to try a face-off [head-on pass], and I did hit the enemy directly in the face and below. The Russian exploded at a distance of some 30 m [32 yds], just as I went under it. The remains of the fighter fell into a swamp.

'At this point there was one Russian at an altitude of 1500 m [4900 ft] who had followed the fight but not got into it. I made it back to our side without that enemy aircraft attacking me even once. Two 20 mm and two 12.7 mm rounds hit my aeroplane, which was MS-622.'

These were Kalima's 10th and 11th victories, making him TLeLv 14's top scorer – indeed, he was the unit's only ace. Twelve days later he was

The first Mörkö-Morane of 1/HLeLv 28, MSv-631 takes off for an interception from Värtsilä, in Karelia, during August 1944. The victory bar signifies a Yak-9 shot down on 16 July 1944 by SSgt Lars Hattinen – the last Morane ace and, actually, the last Finnish ace of World War 2 (*Olli Riekki*)

appointed to lead a group of pilots that went to Germany for nightfighter training, but the detachment returned three months later when Finland withdrew from the war.

On 6 August 1944 all eight Moranes of 2/TLeLv 14 had to fight 19 Airacobras over Ontrosenvaara. One of the Soviet fighters was destroyed, as was a Morane. The squadron's final aerial victory is described here by 1Lt Matti Niinimäki;

'We patrolled over Tahkokoski-Kypärinen at an altitude of 200 m [660 ft] between 1845 hrs and 1930 hrs. As I flew away from the cloud base I saw two Airacobras on the deck, and after an 800 m [2600 ft] dive I managed to fire at one of them at a range of 100 m [110 yds], hitting it and making it dive into the forest at a 45-degree angle. As I pulled up to avoid another pair of Airacobras I saw an aeroplane crash into the woods.

'My aeroplane was MS-629.'

MÖRKÖ MORANE

A major conversion of the MS.406 entailed fitting the aircraft with a captured Russian Klimov M-105P engine. This had the same external measurements as the Hispano-Suiza 12Y31 from which it was developed, but the output of the Soviet engine had been increased from 860 hp to 1100 hp. The prototype was ordered on 22 October 1942, and the M-105 was first installed in MS-631. On 4 February 1943 WO Aarne Siltamäki took the aircraft aloft for the first time. The initial flights were successful and the prototype was due for further development, but there was no hurry because Bf 109Gs began to arrive in Finland only a few weeks later.

Twenty-year-old fighter pilot Sgt Lars Hattinen at Hirvas in front of 1/LeLv 28 Morane MS-317 in the summer of 1943. He claimed all six of his kills during five weeks in the summer of 1944, three of which were the only victories ever credited to the Mörkö Morane (*Author's collection*)

Engineers initially struggled to solve problems with MSv-631's liquid cooling system, but these had been solved by the spring of 1944. Soon after that two more Moranes were converted, and by 21 November 1945 all 41 remaining MS.406s had been modified to MSv.406 standard.

The Mörkö Morane (Ghost Morane), as the MSv.406 was called, had a top speed at sea level of 445 km/h (276 mph), 510 km/h (317 mph) at 4000 m (13,100 ft) and a cruising speed of 410 km/h (255 mph). It could climb to 5000 m (16,400 ft) in eight minutes and had a service ceiling of 10,300 m [33,780 ft]. The fighter's armament consisted of one Mauser MG 151 20 mm cannon between the cylinder banks and one Chatellerault MAC 1934 7.5 mm machine gun in each wing.

FINAL BATTLES

A major offensive by the Soviet Army, which started on 9 June 1944 on the Karelian Isthmus, initially had no effect on LeR 2's sector. Nevertheless, the 2nd and 3rd Flights of HLeLv 28 were combined to form Detachment Sovelius, and it was ordered to transfer to LeR 3. The rapid movement of the frontline in the Karelian Isthmus caused the HQ to order troops at Maaselkä to move closer to the Finnish borders on 17 June. The LeR 2 units were now ordered to retreat, and this was begun on a squadron basis.

Post-Continuation War Mörkö-Morane MSv-633 of HLeLv 21 at Rissala, near Kuopio, where it arrived on 17 March 1945. Two weeks later blue-and-white cockades were painted on the aircraft as demanded by the Allied Supervision Commission, headed by the Soviet Union (Olli Riekki)

On 1 July HLeLv 28 received its first Bf 109G-2 – it was sent ten more during the course of the month. These equipped the 2nd and 3rd Flights, while on 11 July the 1st Flight received its first Mörkö Morane at Värtsilä. Five days later a Mörkö Morane of 1/HLeLv 28 saw action for the first time after SSgt Lars Hattinen was scrambled;

'I took off at 1800 hrs to intercept aeroplanes heading west from Ägläjärvi. At Tolvajärvi I saw four Yak fighters, two at 1000m [3300 ft] and two at 3000 m [9,800 ft], and on the deck I saw six Il-2s. I attacked the lower pair of Yaks, which flew in an agitated manner. They evaded right away and a turning fight ensued, which the upper pair also joined. The aeroplanes were very agile and equal to the MSv, and it was hard to put a bead on them. After some turning around the top pair went for the deck and the other pair attempted to break off eastwards.

'The battle went on for some 15 more minutes, until I got a clean shot at the aeroplane I had first targeted. I gave it a burst, but it kept evading. On the second burst it caught fire and fell into a swamp from 10 m [35 ft]. I tried to get the other Yak, but he had a speed advantage of maybe 20 km/h [12 mph]. It broke off. Then I went after the Il-2 formation flying to one side of me. I fired at them from the side, but my cannon was out of action. I gave them a burst with my wing guns but, knowing they have no effect on Il-2s, I gave up the chase.

'The MSv had proven itself to be equal to the Yak fighter. Although the latter machines were very agile and their pilots skilful in handling them, the Yaks did not get into a firing position during my fight with them.

'When the Il-2s observed me they dived down to the deck and closed up the formation. When I attacked from the side, one turned towards me, firing its frontal cannon. I had obviously interrupted their mission since they seemed to have a lot of ammunition left.

'My aeroplane was MSv-631.'

During the late morning of 30 July, TLeLv 14's Detachment Vuorinen, which was sent to assist HLeLv 28, had to fight more than 30 Russian fighters over Tolvajärvi. One Airacobra was shot down with no losses to the Finns. The Mörkö Morane of 1/HLeLv 28 pilot SSgt Hattinen engaged a Russian formation consisting of about 30 Il-2s escorted by 20+ fighters. Hattinen quickly shot down two Airacobras, but when he went after the ground-attack aircraft their return fire hit his fuel tank and torched MSv-617. Hattinen dived away, pulled up again and bailed out to safety. The two Airacobras credited to Hattinen following this mission made him the last Finn to achieve ace status during the Russo-Finnish conflicts.

All aerial activity had ceased by 10 August, and on 4 September 1944 the commander of the *Ilmavoimat* ordered the air regiments to inform their squadrons that all fighting was to stop at 0700 hrs that day. The ceasefire duly came into effect, and two weeks later this was confirmed by the signing of the Moscow Armistice.

APPENDICES

Appendix 1

Tactical Organisation of *Armée de l'Air* Fighter Units

The basic tactical formation for fighter units was the *patrouille* (patrol), with a leader and two wingmen. The *patrouille* could be broken down in multiple ways – *patrouille double* (six aircraft), *patrouille triple* (nine aircraft) and also *patrouille simple* (two aircraft) or, more subtly, *patrouille simple double* (four aircraft), and any other combinations such as *patrouille double mixte* (eight aircraft). The *chef de patrouille* (patrol leader) was an officer or a seasoned NCO, experience always prevailing over the rank.

French ranks cannot be compared with their RAF counterparts, where ranks and functions fuse into each other. They are closer to the US or German system. Colonel and lieutenant-colonel are easy to translate, with the remaining key commissioned flying ranks being commandant (major), capitaine (captain), lieutenant (1st Lieutenant), sous-lieutenant (2nd Lieutenant) and aspirant (flight officer). Non-commissioned officer ranks are adjudant-chef (warrant officer), adjudant (technical sergeant), sergent-chef (staff sergeant) and sergent (sergeant).

Appendix 2

Acedom – The French way

Readers familiar with this series will not need to have the term 'ace' explained. However, they may be interested to know that at the beginning of the World War 2, to enhance *l'esprit d'équipe*, the Headquarters of the *Armée de l'Air* decided that *all* pilots belonging to a *patrouille* (whatever the number of aircraft involved) should be awarded a full victory. That is why a Bf 109 shot down on 22 November 1939 was confirmed and attributed to no fewer than eight pilots of two different *Groupes*, each one being awarded a full victory (in the USAAF each pilot would have been credited with 0.125 of a victory). Of course, each *Groupe* (GC I/3 and GC II/6) was awarded only one victory, but that was already one too many in the overall total.

Appendix 3

Claims for confirmed victories of *Armée de l'Air* MS.406 units (3 September 1939 to 25 June 1940)

	Claims – Morane only	Claims – grand total	Notes
GC III/1	28	28	Disbanded on 12/8/40
GC I/2	24	24	Disbanded on 7/8/40
GC II/2	17	17	Disbanded on 10/8/40
GC III/2	19	32	Converted to H-75A on 19/5/40
GC I/3	4	52	Converted to D.520 on 7/12/39
GC II/3	4	34	Converted to D.520 on 9/5/40
GC III/3	25	33	Converted to D.520 on 30/5/40
GC I/6	14	14	Disbanded on 15/8/40
GC II/6	10	17	Converted to MB.152 on 18/5/40
GC III/6	11	18	Converted to D.520 on 31/5/40
GC II/7	16	27	Converted to D.520 on 25/5/40
GC III/7	15	15	Converted to D.520 on 22/6/40
Total	**187**	**311**	

Notes
– Shared victories are counted as one for each *Groupe*
– Units in bold fought with the MS.406 until the end of the campaign (25/6/40)

Appendix 4

MS.406 Aces of the *Armée de l'Air*

Pilot	Unit	Morane Kills	Other	Total
Sgt Édouard Le Nigen	GC III/3	12(3)		12
Cne Robert Williame	GC I/2	8(4)		8
Adj Edgar Gagnaire	GC III/1	7(2)		7
Sgt Jacques de Puybusque	GC I/2	7(1)		7
Adj-chef Pierre Dorcy	GC II/2	6(-)		6
Adj Albert Littolff	GC III/7	6(-)	8	14
Sgt Kléber Doublet	GC III/1	6(3)		6
Sous-Lt Henri Raphenne	GC I/6	5(3)		5
Adj-chef Roger Saussol	GC III/1	5(2)		5
Adj Maurice Morey	GC III/2	5(-)		5
Sgt-chef Georges Elmlinger	GC III/2	5(1)	3	8

Note

– Figures in brackets denote the number of victories claimed alone

Appendix 5

MS.406 Aces of the *Ilmavoimat*

Name	Rank*	Unit	Morane score	Total score	Remarks
Urho Lehtovaara	MSgt	2/LLv 28	14	41.5	(MHR)
Martti Inehm	2Lt	2/LLv 28	8	8	MIA 26/12/41
Antti Tani	MSgt	1/LLv 28	7	20.5	
Martti Kalima	Capt	2/TLeLv 14	6.5	11	
Toivo Tomminen	Sgt	3/LLv 28	6.5	6.5	KIA 4/12/41
Aarre Linnamaa	2Lt	1/LLv 28	6	6	KIA 24/4/42
Lars Hattinen	SSgt	1/HLeLv 28	6	6	
Tuomo Hyrkki	Capt	1/LLv 28	5	5	
Pauli Massinen	1Lt	2/LLv 28	5	5	

Appendix 6

Ilmavoimat Aces with MS.406 victories

Name	Rank*	Unit	Morane score	Total score	Remarks
Hemmo Leino	Sgt	1/LeLv 14	3	11	
Paavo Myllylä	1Lt	1/LLv 28	1.5	22	
Aaro Nuorala	Sgt	1/LeLv 14	1.5	14.5	
Veikko Karu	1Lt	3/LLv 28	2	12	(MHR)
Jouko Myllymäki	1Lt	3/LLv 28	2	5	(MIA 25/6/44)

Appendix 7

Notable *Ilmavoimat* pilots with MS.406 victories

Name	Rank*	Unit	Morane score	Total score	Remarks
Reino Turkki	Capt	2/LLv 28	4	4	
Aarne Nissinen	1Lt	3/LLv 28	4	4	KIFA 27/10/41
Oskari Jussila	SSgt	3/LLv 28	4	4	
Auvo Maunula	Maj	E/LeLv 28	2	3	(MHR), KIFA 17/5/44

Notes

* – The rank given is the one held at the time of the last claim. The unit stated is the one in which the majority of Morane victories were scored.

() – Remarks mentioned in parenthesis refer to another unit or another period

MHR – Mannerheim Cross

KIA – Killed in action

KIFA – Killed in flying accident

MIA – Missing in action.

In some instances the victory totals that appear here differ slightly from those published in earlier *Osprey Aircraft of the Aces* volumes, as since they were published in the late 1990s, new information has surfaced from the Russian archives allowing a few claims recorded as damaged to be upgraded to confirmed victories.

1

MS.406C1 N°272 (N-684) of Cne Bernard Challe, CO of the 2nd *Escadrille* of GC I/3, Bruxelles-Evère, July 1939

Bernard was one of the four Challe brothers who all had successful careers in the *Armée de l'Air*. Born in October 1906, he graduated from the prestigious military school at Saint-Cyr and became CO of 2e *Escadrille* of GC I/3 in August 1938, which he gallantly led during the 1940 campaign. Challe achieved a personal score of five victories, three of them while flying the MS.406. During the Vichy years he commanded GC I/3 and GC I/8 before joining the Resistance. He was arrested by the *Gestapo* and sent to the infamous Buchenwald camp in August 1944. In January 1959 *Général de Corps d'Armée Aérienne* (Air Chief Marshal) Bernard Challe played an active part in an attempted coup aimed at seizing power in Algeria. Following its failure his career was abruptly put to an end by Général Charles De Gaulle. Challe died in January 1977.

2

MS.406C1 N°252 (N-664) of Adj Antonin Combette, 1st *Escadrille* of GC I/3, Velaine-en-Haye, 24 September 1939

Antonin Combette claimed the *Armée de l'Air's* fourth victory of the Phoney War, and the first one credited to a Morane pilot on 24 September 1939 when he downed a Bf 109D from 2/JGr. 152 – its pilot, Gefreiter A Hesselbach, was captured. Combette became a most sought-after aviator by war correspondents following his success, and his portrait appeared in many French newspapers and magazines. Combette added three more victories to his tally, the last one while flying a D.520, prior to being shot down and taken prisoner on 15 May 1940.

3

MS.406C1 N°183 (N-503) of Adj-chef Pierre Le Gloan, 5th *Escadrille* of GC III/6, Wez-Thuisy, 26 November 1939

Pierre Le Gloan claimed the first of his 18 victories while flying this aircraft. However, the name *peau d'vache* (bastard), worn on the spine of the fighter, was probably applied by another pilot after Le Gloan had been assigned a brand new aeroplane. He claimed only four kills at the controls of a Morane, and the rest while flying a D.520, including five Italian aeroplanes in the same sortie on 15 June 1940 (a feat for which he was immediately commissioned) and seven British fighters in Syria during June-July 1941. Still with GC III/6 in Algeria after the Allied landings in northern Africa (Operation *Torch*), Le Gloan resumed fighting against the Germans flying P-39s. On 11 September 1943 he forgot to jettison his belly tank before making a forced landing due to engine trouble, and was killed when his Airacobra duly exploded.

4

MS.406C1 N°730 (L-750) of Adj Edgar Gagnaire, 1st *Escadrille* of GC III/1, Velaine-en-Haye, 10 March 1940

Edgar Gagnaire claimed seven victories while flying the MS.406 (five shared) prior to his death on 10 June 1940 (see profile 8 for details). This particular aicraft was shot down in

flames over Anizy-le-Château on 19 May 1940, most likely by Hauptmann Bernhard Mielke, *Staffelkapitän* of 3.(J)/LG 2. Its pilot, Lt Paul Marche, CO of the 1st *Escadrille*, was killed.

5

MS.406C1 N°847 (L-876) of Sous-Lt Henri Raphenne, 1st *Escadrille* of GC I/6, Romilly-sur-Seine, early May 1940

Henri Raphenne claimed five victories (two shared) with the MS.406. He had the dubious honour of being the last *Armée de l'Air* aircrew member to be killed during the campaign, having been shot down by flak at 2035 hrs on 24 June 1940 while on a strafing mission near Romans.

6

MS.406C1 N°686 (L-715) of Cne Robert Williame, CO of the 1st *Escadrille* of GC I/2, Damblain, 27 May 1940

MS.406C1 No 686 was reportedly christened *Juliette II* after the youngest daughter of the Barbier family, whose fields were next to the aerodrome at Beauvais-Tillé that was occupied by GC I/2 just prior to the declaration of war. This particular aircraft was the second MS.406 allotted to Robert Williame (see profile 10 for his biographical details), and it was lost when Damblain airfield was strafed by Bf 109s on 21 May 1940.

7

MS.406C1 N°795 (L-824) of Adj-chef Jean Bertrand, 6th *Escadrille* of GC III/7, Orly, 31 May 1940

Jean Bertrand was shot down by Bf 109s from I./JG 3 and III./JG 53 over Abbeville at 1835 hrs on 31 May while flying this aircraft. His hands and face already badly burned by the time he took to his parachute, Bertrand was sent to hospital. Following his recovery, he subsequently resumed flying, only to be killed in an accident in August 1944. Bertrand had claimed three victories, all Hs 126s shared with other pilots, on 14 May 1940.

8

MS.406C1 N°846 (L-875) of Adj Edgar Gagnaire, 1st *Escadrille* of GC III/1, Rozay-en-Brie, 8 June 1940

Edgar Gagnaire claimed seven victories while flying the MS.406 (five shared) prior to his death on 10 June 1940. He fell victim to German flak at GC III/1's recently captured airfield at Rozay-en-Brie after flying low and slow to 'show the roundels' to French soldiers in accordance with orders. Unbeknown to Gagnaire and his squadronmates, their airfield had been overrun by advancing German forces shortly after they had departed Rozay-en-Brie on a patrol (in which they had shared in the destruction of an Hs 126).

9

MS.406C1 N°777 (L-806) of Sgt Kléber Doublet, 2nd *Escadrille* of GC III/1, Norrent-Fontes, early June 1940

Kléber Doublet was one of the few true MS.406 aces, although three of his six victories were shared with other pilots. Left behind at Connantre because of a mechanical failure to his fighter when GC III/1 was sent to a less exposed airfield on 10 June, Doublet had his legs crushed during an air raid by Do 17s on Norrent-Fontes the following day. He succumbed to his wounds on 12 June.

10

MS.406C1 N°966 (no buzz number) of Cne Robert Williame, CO of the 1st *Escadrille* of GC I/2, Dijon-Longvic, June 1940

Robert Williame, born in 1911, was a charismatic leader known for his cheerful nature and his witty remarks, but also for his skill as a fighter pilot. On 11 September 1937 – the 20th anniversary of the death of French World War 1 ace Charles Guynemer – Williame took command of the 1st *Escadrille* of GC I/2, heirs of the prestigious 'Stork' squadron. He claimed eight kills (half of them shared) in two days during the Battle of France – two on 5 June 1940 and the other six 72 hours later. In October 1940, following the armistice, Williame was posted to GC III/9 as the new 2nd *Escadrille* commander after recovering from a bout of scarlet fever. On 31 October, in a mock dogfight with his CO, and probably insufficiently recovered from his illness, Williame lost control of his MB.152 and crashed to his death.

11

MS.406C1 N°288 (N-700) of Sgt Jacques de Puybusque, 1st *Escadrille* of GC I/2, Nîmes-Courbessac, late June 1940

Jacques de Puybusque claimed seven victories (six shared) flying the MS.406. He died in a flying accident in June 1941.

12

MS.406C1 N°307 (N-725) of Cne Pierre Pouyade, CO of *Escadrille* 2/595, Tong, Indochina, early 1942

Born in 1911, Pierre Pouyade took part in the Battle of France as the pilot of a Potez 631. Transferring to Indochina in December 1940, he escaped to China in a Potez 25TOE in October 1942 and joined the *Normandie-Niémen* regiment on the Russian Front, which he led from July 1943 to December 1944. Pouyade personally claimed six victories flying Yak fighters. After the war he had long military and diplomatic careers, before passing away in September 1970. His Morane, shown here, wears the specific markings adopted after an incident in January 1942, when three Japanese Ki-27s shot down three Moranes in error, killing one pilot and wounding another.

13

MS.406C1 N°842 (L-871) of Lt Michel Laurant, *Groupe Aérien Mixte*, Diego Arrachart, Madagascar, 7 May 1942

Michel Laurant force landed in this aircraft on 7 May 1942 during the only aerial combat of the entire Madagascar campaign (Operation *Ironclad*). The MS.406s had been engaged by Martlets of 881 NAS flying from HMS *Illustrious*.

14

Yak-9D N°434 of Cne Albert Littolff, *Groupe Normandie*, Khationki, Soviet Union, July 1943

Albert Littolff, aged 29, flew his D.520 to England on 25 June 1940 to become one of the early Free French fighter pilots, and one of the most successful. Having claimed six victories flying MS.406s with GC III/7 during the Battle of France, he was subsequently credited with eight more kills – four in the desert (flying Hurricanes) and four in Russia (flying Yak-9s). Littolff was first incorporated into the *Groupe de Chasse* No 1 at Ismailia, in Egypt, in April 1941. He then flew with *Groupe Alsace* until April 1942, but did not score with the latter unit. Volunteering to join the *escadrille* (then *Groupe*) *Normandie* on the Russian

Front, Littolff took part in the hard early aerial combats around Kursk and was listed as missing in action on 16 July 1943 after having claimed his 14th, and final, kill over Krasnikovo. His body was found many years later and returned to France in 1960.

15

Yak-9D of Lt Léon Cuffaut, *Régiment Normandie*, Toula, Soviet Union, December 1943

Léon Cuffaut was one of the *Armée de l'Air's* most colourful characters. Born in 1911, he was a sous-lieutenant with GC II/6 when war broke out. Cuffaut claimed two Bf 109s (shared) from I./JG 76 on 22 November 1939 and was then transferred to the *Centre d'Instruction à la Chasse* (an operational training unit for fighter pilots) at Chartres as an instructor. Seeing further action with GC II/3 in Syria in June 1941, Cuffaut returned to the Allied fold later that year. He subsequently volunteered to join *Groupe Normandie* on the Russian Front, reaching the unit in December 1943. Cuffaut participated in the hard combats over East Prussia in September-October 1944, where, in little more than a month, he claimed 11 victories (six shared) and three probables (two shared). Physically exhausted, Cuffaut was sent back to France after being shot down on 27 October. He resumed fighting in Indochina between July 1953 and September 1955, and finally retired in January 1962 with the rank of *Général de Brigade* (Air Vice-Marshal), having amassed 8460 flying hours in no fewer than 1010 operational sorties – a French record.

16

Spitfire Mk VB EP813 flown by Cne Georges Valentin, CO of 1st *Escadrille* of the GC II/7 (No 326 'French' Sqn) *Nice*, Ajaccio, Corsica, July 1944

One of the most gifted French fighter pilots, Georges Valentin, aged 32, started World War 2 as a sergent-chef and was commissioned at the end of 1939. He claimed seven victories during the May-June 1940 campaign (but only three with the Morane), and added an RAF Blenheim in November 1940 and two more German bombers in late 1943, after GC II/7 had been re-equipped with Spitfires and had rejoined the war on the Allied side as No 326 'French' Sqn. Valentin was killed by flak over Dijon on 8 September 1944. All but two of his ten victories were shared. The Spitfire shown here wears the pilot's initial, as was the custom with the 1st *Escadrille* of GC II/7. EP813 was a late-build Spitfire VB fitted with a Merlin 46 engine that had been handed over to the French by the USAAF.

17

MS.406C1 MS-325/'Yellow 2' of Cpl Toivo Tomminen, 3/LLv 28, Naarajärvi, June 1941

MS-325 was the first aircraft assigned to 21-year-old Cpl Toivo Tomminen, and, piloting this machine, he claimed his first kill (an SB bomber) on 14 July 1941. Tomminen became an ace on 19 October 1941 when he downed an I-153 and an R-Z in MS-315. Promoted to sergeant, he was killed in action on 4 December 1941 when, flying his last assigned aircraft, MS-329, he was struck by Hurricane IIB BD761 from 152nd IAP. The pilot of the latter machine, Snr Lt Nikolay F Repnikov, also perished in the deliberate head-on ramming attack. Tomminen's final score was 6.5 kills.

18

MS.406C1 MS-603/'Yellow 7' of 1Lt Jouko Myllymäki, 3/LLv 28, Naarajärvi, June 1941

1Lt Jouko Myllymäki made his first Morane kill in the Winter War when he downed an I-16 on 9 March 1940. He flew MS-603 until the end of 1941, scoring one confirmed and one probable with it. Myllymäki then spent nine months as an instructor until he was posted as a captain to command 2/LeLv 24 on 11 September 1943. He scored three more victories with the Bf 109G-2, but was posted missing in action on 25 June 1944 at the age of 28, with a final tally of five victories.

19

MS.406C1 MS314/'White 4' of 1Lt Pauli Massinen, 2/LLv 28, Karkunranta, September 1941

MS314 was assigned to 2/LLv 28 deputy leader 1Lt Pauli Massinen for his entire tour in the Continuation War, which ended on 7 November 1941 when he was ordered to the rear to serve as an instructor. Massinen had claimed his first kill (in MS318) during the Winter War on 2 March 1940, and he became an ace on 21 August 1941. His tally included a flying boat and four bombers. Unlike other pilots in his flight, Massinen chose not to mark the victories on the fin of his Morane. This aircraft continued to serve with LLv 28 until it was listed as missing in action on 4 July 1944.

20

MS.406C1 MS-317/'Black 2' of 2Lt Paavo Myllylä, 1/LLv 28, Solomanni, October 1941

This aircraft was delivered to the unit on 3 September 1941 following repairs undertaken at the State Aircraft Factory, and it was assigned to 23-year-old reservist 2Lt Paavo Myllylä. By the end of the year Myllylä had claimed 1.5 confirmed victories with MS-317, and two damaged while flying other Moranes. On 9 February 1943 he was posted as a first lieutenant to LeLv 34, where he began scoring steadily with the Bf 109G. By the cessation of hostilities Myllylä had increased his total to 22 confirmed aerial victories and ten damaged.

21

MS.406C1 MS327/'White 9' of MSgt Urho Lehtovaara, 2/LLv 28, Viitana, November 1941

MSgt Urho Lehtovaara was the MS.406 'ace of aces', scoring 14 confirmed victories. He claimed his first kill (in MS326) in the Winter War on 2 March 1940 when he downed an SB bomber. Lehtovaara's regular machine for the first six months of the Continuation War was MS327, and he claimed five victories with it. This aircraft was destroyed on 23 December 1941 when it caught fire while its engine was being warmed up by blowtorches. Note the ten victory bars on the fighter's fin, the last three (all I-16s) of which Lehtovaara had claimed on 9 September 1941. At that point he was Finland's joint top scorer with WOs Oiva Tuominen and Ilmari Juutilainen.

22

MS.406C1 MS318/'White 2' of 2Lt Martti Inehmo, 2/LLv 28, Viitana, December 1941

Reservist 2Lt Martti Inehmo was the second-highest scorer in MS.406s, with eight confirmed victories. He opened his tally in the Winter War by downing a DB-3 bomber (in MS304) on 11 March 1940 – this proved to be the last kill of the conflict.

MS318 was Inehmo's second assigned aircraft of the Continuation War, but he claimed no kills with it. Inehmo failed to return from a mission to Maaselkä in poor weather on 26 December 1941, the ace flying MS-618 at the time of his demise.

23

MS.406C1 MS-304 of MSgt Urho Lehtovaara, 3/LLv 28, Solomanni, March 1942

Posted to 3/LLv 28 for a six-month tour in December 1941, MSgt Urho Lehtovaara was assigned MS-304. He downed three I-16s with this machine on 9 September 1941 to bring his Continuation War tally to ten kills. Lehtovaara later added three more victories with the Morane prior to being posted to LeLv 34 on 28 March 1943, where he increased his score to 41.5 flying Bf 109Gs. Finland's fourth-ranking ace, Lehtovaara was awarded the Mannerheim Cross on 9 July 1944.

24

MS.406C1 MS-607/'Black 1' of 2Lt Aarre Linnamaa, 1/LLv 28, Solomanni, March 1942

After flying MS-308 as his assigned aircraft, six-victory ace 2Lt Aarre Linnamaa was given MS-607 in December 1941 – he had previously claimed two SB bombers with it on 12 September. On 24 April 1942 he had to make a forced landing in enemy territory. When close to friendly lines Linnamaa stepped on a mine and was wounded. When he heard the voices of an approaching patrol he shot himself rather than be captured. Unfortunately for 23-year-old Linnamaa, the patrol turned out to be Finnish.

25

MS.406C1 MS-606/'White 5' of 1Lt Reino Turkki, 2/LLv 28, Viitana, March 1942

1Lt Reino Turkki led 2/LLv 28 from the Winter War until the end of October 1943, when, following his promotion to captain, he was put in charge of 1/LeLv 28 for the rest of the war. Turkki's tally included four confirmed victories and two damaged, the first in the Winter War. He flew MS-606 until October 1942 and then MS-626. After the war Turkki remained in the service, rising to the rank of general lieutenant and commanding the *Ilmavoimat* from 1964. He died on 6 December 1968, aged 55.

26

MS.406C1 MS-619/'White 5' of MSgt Antti Tani, 1/LeLv 28, Solomanni, August 1942

Twenty-year-old Sgt Antti Tani scored his and his squadron's first victory – an SB bomber – on 25 June 1941, flying MS-311 as his first assigned aeroplane. In October 1941 he was allocated MS-619, which he flew until posted to LeLv 34 on 15 April 1943 to fly Bf 109Gs. Tani's Morane tally was six confirmed victories, including two Pe-2 bombers in MS-619, and three damaged. Later, he raised his score to 20.5 confirmed kills and five damaged.

27

MS.406C1 MS328/'Black 8' of Sgt Martti Vihinen, 1/LeLv 28, Solomanni, March 1943

Four different pilots used this aircraft to score five victories, which were duly marked on its fin. In 1940-41, while still in French camouflage but wearing these markings, MS328 had been the assigned aircraft of flight leader 1Lt Tuomo Hyrkki.

A five-victory ace, one of his claims to fame was that he scored the first Morane victory in the Winter War – a DB-3 bomber – on 17 February 1940. At that time the Moranes were armed with only three 7.5 mm machine guns.

28
MS.406C1 MS-615/'Blue X' of Maj Auvo Maunula, LeLv 28, Hirvas, March 1943

Maj Auvo Maunula was both a reconnaissance and fighter pilot in the Winter War, flying with LLv 12. In the early stages of the Continuation War he led LLv 12, and he scored a victory with a Fokker D.XXI on 19 February 1942. For his reconnaissance and leadership achievements Maunula was awarded the Mannerheim Cross on 8 September 1942 – three weeks after he had been posted to command LeLv 28. Maunula added two more Morane victories before being killed in a flying accident on 17 May 1944, aged 36.

29
MS.406C1 MS-319/'White 9' of Sgt Hemmo Leino, 1/LeLv 14, Tiiksjärvi, early March 1943

Sgt Hemmo Leino scored victories with the Fokker D.XXI, MS.406 and Bf 109G, accumulating 11 kills. Leino's first Morane kill came on 5 November 1942 when he downed a LaGG-3, and he added two I-15bis to his tally on 16 March 1943. These were subsequently marked on the rudder of MS-319 – Leino had previously claimed 1.5 kills with the D.XXI. Most of his victories were scored in June and July 1944, flying the Bf 109G-6.

30
MS.406C1 MS-611/'White 11' of Sgt Aaro Nuorala, 1/LeLv 14, Tiiksjärvi, March 1943

Like Sgt Hemmo Leino, Sgt Aaro Nuorala flew with LLv 10, LeLv 14 and LeLv 34 and scored victories with the same three types of fighter, racking up a tally of 14.5 aerial victories. His first Morane kill came in MS-611 on 16 March 1943 (an I-15bis), and a week later he added a shared victory (an I-16) to his tally. Nuorala's 'high season' was also in June and July 1944, flying the Bf 109G-6.

31
MS.406C1 MS-622/'Red 2' of Capt Martti Kalima,

2/TLeLv 14, Tiiksjärvi, June 1944

The top scorer in South Viena, close to the White Sea, Capt Martti Kalima claimed 11 victories. Before converting to the Morane he had scored four victories flying the D.XXI. Kalima scored LeLv 14's first MS.406 victory on 5 November 1943, claiming a LaGG-3. His last victories came on 2 June 1944, when, as the leader of 2/TLeLv 14, he claimed two LaGG-3s in this aircraft – Kalima had previously downed two LaGG fighters in MS-622 in April and May. He then led a group of Finnish pilots to Germany for nightfighter training, but returned after the ceasefire between Finland and the USSR came into effect on 4 September 1944.

32
Mörkö Morane MSv-631/'White 1' of SSgt Lars Hattinen, 1/HLeLv 28, Värtsilä, July 1944

Only three Mörkö Moranes reached the frontline during the Continuation War, MSv-631 being the first, on 11 July 1944. It was occasionally flown by SSgt Lars Hattinen, the last ace to emerge in this conflict. He was also the only pilot with claims flying the Mörkö Morane. Hattinen already had four 'regular' Morane victories to his name when he scored the first (a Yak-1) with MSv-631 on 16 July 1944. He added a double (two Airacobras) exactly two weeks later with MSv-617, a though he was also shot down himself and parachuted to safety.

——— BIBLIOGRAPHY ———

Ehrengardt, Christian-Jacques and Listement, Philippe, *Les Pilotes de Chasse Francais 39–45* (Aero-Editions, 1999).
Keskinen, Kalevi and Stenman, Kari, *Aerial Victories* Vols 1 and 2 (K Stenman, 2006).
Keskinen, Kalevi and Stenman, Kari, *Morane-Saulnier MS.406* (K Stenman, 2005).
Keskinen, Kalevi and Stenman, Kari, *LeR 2* (K Stenman, 2001).
Keskinen, Kalevi and Stenman, Kari, *LeR 1* (K Stenman, 2002).
Rédaction d'Avions, *Le Morane-Saulnier 406* (Lela Presse, 1998).
Stenman, Kari and Keskinen, Kalevi, *Osprey Aircraft of the Aces 23 – Finnish Aces of World War 2* (Osprey Publishing, 1998).

INDEX